MEDITATION
week by week

David Fontana

MEDITATION

52 meditations to help you grow in peace
and awareness

DUNCAN BAIRD PUBLISHERS
LONDON

Meditation Week by Week
David Fontana

Distributed in the USA and Canada by
Sterling Publishing Co., Inc.
387 Park Avenue South
New York, NY 10016-8810

This edition first published in the UK and USA
in 2004 by Duncan Baird Publishers Ltd
Sixth Floor, Castle House
75–76 Wells Street
London W1T 3QH

Managing Editor: Julia Charles
Editor: Zoë Stone
Managing Designer: Manisha Patel
Designer: Allan Sommerville

Library of Congress Cataloging-in-Publication
Data Available

ISBN-13: 978-1-84483-406-8
ISBN-10: 1-84483-406-9
10 9 8 7 6 5 4 3 2 1

Typeset in Palatino
Color reproduction by Scanhouse, Malaysia
Printed and bound in Thailand by Imago

For information about custom editions, special sales,
premium and corporate purchases, please contact
Sterling Special Sales Department at 800-805-5489 or
specialsales@sterlingpub.com.

Contents

Introduction

The title of this book does not imply that one of the 52 meditations should be attempted every seven days. Meditation isn't that kind of practice. Individuals vary in their rate of progress, and in any case many of the meditations are intended to be practised for as long as you continue meditating, rather than be attempted once or twice and then left behind. Work at your own pace.

The practical sections of this book are referred to as meditations throughout, although certain of the earlier ones in Chapter 1 are in the nature of introductory exercises. Chapter 1 gives you the background to meditation and these introductory meditations are important. One of the reasons many people give up meditation practice is that they come to it unprepared. The remaining chapters deal with the practicalities and development of meditation. I recommend that you follow the meditations in the order that they appear in the book, but this is not essential – circumstances may not allow you to work on one or other of them on first reading, and you may wish to return to it later. You may sometimes find it necessary to concentrate on just one meditation for some time until you derive benefit from it. And you may wish to read the book right through, to get the feel of it, before you undertake any of the meditations. It is your book, and you must use it as you think best.

A year seems a long time, but there is an old saying that in meditation time means nothing. So in the year ahead put aside conventional ideas of progress, of measuring how far you have travelled each week and each month. Notice instead how sometimes you seem to come a long way in a single meditation session, while at other times you may feel you're slipping back even beyond your starting point. Do not be elated by the first kind of experience or disappointed by the second. These observations are essential lessons about your mind. Distracting emotions, such as elation and disappointment, are part of the obstacles that have to be overcome on the path to self-discovery.

During meditation even the sense of time can change. Some sessions may seem shorter or longer than they actually are, or even seem to take place outside time, so that the clock loses its meaning, and you learn how subjective is our sense of time.

This book is not written from the perspective of any one of the spiritual traditions, and if more mention is made of some traditions than others, this is merely because they lay most emphasis upon meditation.

When you reach the end of the book, use it for reference purposes – it is all too easy to forget what we have learned. I hope you will have discovered that meditation is for you, just as it is for everyone (though too few realize it). But provided that the book has at least helped to set you on the path, it will have done its job.

Beginning Self-Awareness

- *What is Meditation?*
- *Why Meditate?*
- *Your State of Being: Where Are You Now?*
- *Your Physical Self*
- *Movement and Stillness*
- *Your Mental Self*
- *The Whole You*
- *Beginning Sitting Meditation*
- *A Time and Place to Sit*
- *What to Wear*
- *The Moving World*
- *Absorbing the World*
- *The Sleeping Self*
- *Meditation and Spirituality*
- *Meditation and Ethical Behaviour*

Self-awareness begins in the third year of life. Before this phase of life, we are driven by physical needs (food, drink, comfort) and by intuitive reactions (fear, interest, pleasure). But with a dawning sense of self there comes the recognition of personal likes and dislikes, and the drive to make decisions and demands in order to satisfy them. From this time onward, we grow increasingly autonomous. The way in which the self develops depends very much upon temperament and upon life experiences.

The self is therefore, from an early age, our companion in life. The way in which we think of ourselves, and the way in which others think of us, help determine the person we become. But how self-aware are we? How well do we know ourselves? What degree of control do we have over ourselves? What practices do we have for being more objective about ourselves – for changing those things in ourselves that we dislike? The self is a dynamic process and life events are constantly changing the way in which we see ourselves. Can we take responsibility for this process of change, or are we largely at the mercy of whatever life brings? Meditation is a way of answering some of these questions.

What is Meditation?

Meditation is the direct experience of your own mind. How surprising you may say. Surely we are continually experiencing our own minds? Not so. For most of our waking lives we experience only the thoughts, emotions and sensations that fill our minds, an ever-changing stream of distractions – joyful and sad, welcome and unwelcome. This fleeting flow of thoughts and impressions is no more the mind than the water in a cup is the cup. In meditation, we distance ourselves from this flow instead of identifying with it. We become an observer instead of a participant. And as the practice develops, so the flow becomes a trickle, sometimes ceasing altogether – if only briefly, enabling us to recognize that the mind is still there even when thoughts are not. Instead of distractions, there is a calm, clear awareness, a sense of being instead of doing, of tranquility instead of confusion.

If meditation sounds like entering into a light trance, nothing could be further from the truth. Meditation is a state of poised alertness, not one of drowsy forgetfulness. As the mind settles into meditation, it frees itself from the exhausting effects of its own mental chatter. The mind becomes concentrated and focused, and after the meditation it remains calm and refreshed. And if the practice of meditation seems like withdrawal from the world into an introverted state that cuts us off from fellow beings, this isn't so. Meditation, by helping to free the mind from an excessive concern with its own restless chatter, enables us to be more aware of others, more conscious of their needs, and better able to relate warmly and compassionately to them. By assisting the development of concentration, meditation also allows us to act more efficiently and effectively in the world, and to meet the challenges of daily life with greater clarity and equanimity.

Often, it is supposed that meditation requires sitting on a cushion in a quiet, still room. This again is a misapprehension. Certainly a daily session of quiet sitting is essential for progress, but even in the early days of practice it is possible to meditate at suitable moments during the day – for example, while travelling by train, waiting to meet a friend, or taking a walk. A few minutes of meditation can help to calm the nerves before a stressful event such as public speaking, and to refresh the mind after a tiring (or tiresome!) meeting or after a hard day's work.

All the great spiritual traditions have placed major emphasis upon meditation as a path to personal growth. In recent years psychologists have also recognized its value as a method of relaxation and of mind training. For many people in the East meditation is a normal way of life from early childhood onward, and although the practice suffered neglect in the West for some centuries, all the techniques taught in the East are now once more being actively and widely taught in Western traditions.

Why Meditate?

Meditation is less the discovery of a new skill, than the re-discovery of a natural state of mind that is always there and has always been there, behind the surface chatter that usually claims our attention. One of the best ways of illustrating why we should meditate is to think of a crowded and cluttered room, a room in which we are always trying to find space for new things, while we are reluctant to throw out the old. A room in which we are continually falling over things heaped on the floor, where we can never sit down without having to remove things from the chairs, and a room where we can never find what we want without a frustrating and time-consuming search.

Now think of the same room with much of the unwanted clutter removed, a room in which we can now operate with greater ease and much less stress. A room where we can enjoy the colours and the decor, a room in which it is now a pleasure to sit and relax. The room is of course our own mind, and the transformation in the room is the result of meditation.

Meditation is thus a form of mental spring-cleaning, or if you prefer, a form of mental purification. It rests and relaxes the mind, develops powers of concentration and awareness, helps us deal with daily challenges with greater equanimity, and assists us to operate more efficiently and effectively. But it goes much further than this. In a real sense, we are most of us strangers to ourselves. Faced with the hectic pressures of modern living, we have little time for self-reflection, and even less time to experience who we are – what lies behind the surface activity that occupies so much of our attention. So meditation is also a path toward self-knowledge. It allows us to see into ourselves, almost as if a window, hitherto obscured with dust, has been wiped clean. For many people, this process is spiritual as well as psychological. We learn that there is more to us than our material selves, more than a mortal brain and a mortal body.

These are reasons enough for learning to meditate, but there are also physical benefits. As the mind becomes calmer, so the body learns also to relax, to re-discover its equilibrium. As we become better able to handle stress, and better able to experience the wellbeing that comes with tranquility, so there is often a reduction in blood pressure and in heart-rate that persists even outside meditation. Released from tensions, the body seems better able to ward off infections and perhaps also other illnesses. There is evidence that regular meditators may live longer than non-meditators, and evidence that they take more pleasure in the natural world, in the beauties of the earth and sky.

Meditation may also help in pain control and in healing. It is thus a form of treatment that is free and has, for the very great majority of people, no side-effects or contra-indications.

Your State of Being: Where Are You Now?

We live in a highly extroverted world. For most of our waking life our attention is directed outward – to the workplace, to the television screen, to newspapers and magazines, to films and videos, to canned music, to the noise of traffic and to the voices and demands of other people. We are bombarded by information, things to read, things to know, things to argue about. It is said that a single issue of the *New York Times* contains more pieces of information in its pages than an educated 18th-century man or woman would have met with in a whole lifetime. Small wonder that we have little or no time to stop and look inward and address the vital mystery that accompanies us each day of our lives, the mystery of who and what we are.

So the question "where are you now?" refers to where you are within yourself. For much of our lives, particularly during the formative years of our childhood, other people have been trying to tell us who we are. And on occasions these voices may be conflicting. We have grown up with a bewildering number of labels that other people have chosen to tie upon us. Parents and teachers, friends, partners, colleagues, politicians, marketing executives, theologians, bank managers, biologists and physicists have all tried to tell us whether we are good or bad, clever or slow, beautiful or plain, left or right wing, successful or unsuccessful, sensitive or insensitive, thrifty or extravagant, unselfish or selfish and so on. Although we are right to take some heed of what others tell us, for we live in a social world, the only person who can really know you is you yourself. You are your own expert.

The question "where are you now?" is designed to ask you to think a little about yourself – not in terms of worldly success but in terms of your state of being. Have you come to believe in all the labels others have chosen to fasten on you, or can you discriminate between them? Are you at peace with yourself, and at home in your own mind? Are you aware of the pattern of your thoughts, of the things that preoccupy your mind? Are your thoughts under your control or out of your control? Who is in charge within your mind, you or the mental chatter that insists on returning to things you would rather forget, on past arguments and embarrassments, on vain wishes and longings, on unproductive fantasies? Are you aware of who or what you are behind this chatter? The fact that we should exist at all is a miracle. What do you know about the miracle that is yourself? Are you able to turn away from all distractions, if only for a moment, and reflect upon the experience of actually being alive?

Meditation is a method to help you do just that.

Your Physical Self

Not only do we have no real time to look inward, we have no real time to pay proper attention to what is going on around us. Surrounded as we are by so much frantic activity in the outer world, this may sound a paradoxical thing to say. But it is precisely because this activity is so frantic that we have little time to pay proper attention to any one thing. The sheer volume of things clamouring for our attention and the haste with which each replaces the last means that we are always being pulled away to look or listen to something else, rather like a small child being hurried around a toy shop by an adult in a rush. Thus we are rarely fully in our environment, with time to appreciate the subtle flow of events, the play of colours, textures and shapes, the harmony and the discord with which our fellow men and women arrange the world.

To complicate things further, even when we do have time to experience something properly, we immediately attach concepts to it. We name it and define it, we judge it and value it, we categorize it, often taking it out of context in the process so that the world is experienced as isolated units instead of as a subtle unity of inter-relationships composed of objects and the spaces around them. We don't really experience what it is we are seeing, only our thoughts about it. The diet of constant novelty served up by the

MEDITATION 1: **Become Conscious of the Environment**

It is valuable to see what full attention to our environment feels like. Read through the meditation, and then try it outdoors.

1   *Sit comfortably, and allow your eyes to travel around the garden or open space in which you are sitting. Try to avoid thinking about what you are seeing while you do this. Simply look. Take in the colours, the shapes, of everything you see, and the relation of each object to its surroundings, including the empty space surrounding and defining it. Don't forget to look up and down as well as from side to side. Look at the panorama around you as if seeing it for the first time. Don't label or judge anything you see. If thoughts come to mind, try gently to let them go.*

2   *Now switch attention to your hearing. Focus upon sounds, without trying to identify them. Then do the same with tactile sensations – the warmth of the sun, the feel of the breeze, the touch of the grass.*

3   *Finally, try to take in sight, sounds and sensations all together; again try not to allow thoughts to intrude.*

What effect did this experience have upon you? Did you feel more unity and harmony with the environment? Did you feel it closer to you or more remote? Simply note these effects. There are no right and wrong answers.

media grows stale, leaving us restless and satiated. Imprisoned as most of us are within a man-made environment, we miss the subtle changes presented to us by nature, where each scene not only flows into the next, but changes as the days and weeks and seasons follow each other.

Meditation teaches us once more to look at and take in the world around us. When a famous Buddhist meditation teacher was once asked the secret of meditation he wrote the symbol for attention. Surely there must be more to it than that, persisted his questioner. Once more he wrote attention. Attention not only to one's own mind when sitting in meditation, but properly focused attention on whatever comes into awareness, moment by moment. The present moment is all that we have, and when it passes it is as irrecoverable as the first moment of time. Meditation helps us to engage with the present moment, and to look upon it and the experiences it brings to us as a precious gift.

This state of attention brings with it a much deeper sense of being alive, of being fully here, of an experience of oneness with everything around us. In consequence it has the practical benefit of improving our memory. One reason we forget things so easily is that we fail to pay proper attention to them in the first place. As we learn through meditation to focus more upon our direct experience, so we find it increasingly easy to recall the details of this experience.

MEDITATION 2: **Become Conscious of Your Body**

For much of the time we are only partly conscious of our own bodies. Tensions and bad habits build up unnoticed and remain with us over the years, putting strains upon our muscles, tendons and joints. We lose the sense of the body working as a single, harmonious unit. All too often, one part of it works against the other. Meditation helps redirect our attention to our own bodies, enabling us, when sitting, walking or standing, to become aware of these tensions and bad habits. We can then begin to let them go. Try each of the following meditations over the next few days.

- *Bend to pick up an imaginary object from the floor. Did you bend stiffly? Did your arm reach out while your back preferred to stay upright and thus bent only grudgingly?*

- *Think about your movements while walking or running. Are they uncoordinated, or do they retain the fluidity you had as a child?*

- *Watch how adolescents and young adults move. What do you think of their postures? Notice the large numbers whose shoulders already sag, and whose heads are pulled awkwardly upright in order to look ahead. Notice how many people look as if walking is an unwelcome chore. Look at your own reflection as you pass a shop window. Are there any similarities?*

Movement and Stillness

The whole of nature is characterized by movement and stillness – the movement of wind and water, the stillness of rocks and great works of art; the vigorous upthrust of buds in Spring, the dormancy of seeds in the ground during Winter. Meditation enhances the quality of both movement and stillness. However, our image of the meditator is more often associated with the latter – the Buddhist monk on his cushion in the quiet monastery, the yoga teacher holding her graceful *asana*, the Christian saint kneeling in silent adoration of the divine.

Try to make the body consciousness developed in Meditation 2 a part of daily life. Physical tensions and uneconomic ways of moving not only place unnecessary strains and stresses upon the body, they affect the mind as well. The mind and the body are so closely linked that tensions in the mind quickly reflect themselves in the body, while tensions in the body send messages to the mind that it too should be tense. Try to develop an awareness not only of the body when moving but of the body when still. How many of us can really sit still for any length of time? And how many of us can sit still in a good posture that places no unnecessary strain on any part of the body? Just as physical tensions stress the mind, so physical, relaxed stillness calms the mind.

MEDITATION 3: **Become Conscious of Stillness**

This meditation is intended to help you become aware of tensions and bad posture while experiencing stillness.

1 *Start the practice of stillness by finding a comfortable place to sit, with the back upright and the hands held loosely in the lap or placed palms down on the knees. Sway gently from side to side three times, then come upright and remain still.*

2 *Do you feel any inclination to move? If so, focus upon it. Is it associated with some part of the body – perhaps a feeling of discomfort, or is it a general restlessness? Why is stillness a problem? When you have decided why you want to move, gently try to let the feeling go and remain still.*

3 *Now allow your awareness to travel round the body. Start with the feet, then move upward to the crown of the head. Do this slowly. Notice what you find. Do you feel in touch with every part of your body? Are there tensions anywhere? Can you let them go?*

4 *Remain still for a minute or two after finishing the meditation.*

Your Mental Self

When people are asked where they "live" in their bodies, most Westerners identify a place in the head – usually just behind the eyes. It is often supposed that this is because the brain, the control unit of the body, is in the head. But in fact, the consciousness – the conscious aspect of our minds – can be located almost anywhere in the body (in Eastern cultures, when asked the same question, a sizeable number of people point to the solar plexus, or to the heart). When you stroke a cat, the conscious sensation is located in your hand, not in your head. Similarly, when you hurt your toe, the conscious sensation is located not in the head but in the toe. And when you slide into a warm bath, the conscious sensation is everywhere except in the head.

Meditations 2 and 3 help you become more aware that consciousness really has no set place within the body. By artificially locating it in the head (the habit becomes so strong it's hard to break) we not only distance ourselves from our bodies, we limit the scope of our consciousness. The incessant mental chatter in our heads further limits things. Meditation helps to broaden consciousness once more, ultimately perhaps to allow it to reach out until we feel it embraces the whole of creation.

The feeling of reaching out is not irrational. The outside world is only experienced when we embrace it with our consciousness.

MEDITATION 4: **Become Conscious of Your Mind**

Meditation is about attention, about watching. The meditator identifies what to watch, then watches it steadily throughout the meditation session. Anything can be the object of this watching, including the coming and going of thoughts themselves. Meditation 4 gives you a taste of this form of mind exploration.

1   *Sit comfortably as usual, with the back upright, and turn your attention upon your thoughts. Don't try to think of anything in particular. Just watch what arises.*

2   *Don't hang on to any of the thoughts, whether pleasant or unpleasant. Don't interfere with them or judge them. Watch them come and go, as you would a river flowing under a bridge.*

3   *Continue the meditation for five minutes, longer if you wish.*

What did you notice about your thoughts? Were they trivial or profound? Did they lead from one to another? How many of them involved memories? Were the thoughts familiar ones, as if from your preconscious, or did some of them surprise you? Were there memories that hadn't come to mind for years? Were there some sudden insights or visions that seemed to come from a deeper level? Repeat the meditation from time to time when you are in different moods. What do you learn about your mind?

Reality for each of us literally plays itself out within our own minds. The mind in this sense is limitless. It can reach out to the furthest visible star or register the existence of the smallest grain of sand. Even those things not directly experienced in any given moment can be called to mind through memory and through visualization. In fact, even things never experienced can be imagined, constructed by the mind through its unique creative ability.

In meditation, the mind can lose many of the constraints that we have imposed upon it. Even the boundaries constructed between the conscious and the unconscious parts of the mind can fade, so that the awareness of self deepens to take in not only the surface of our lives but all that we are and all that we have been and will be. This sounds suspiciously mystical, but the mystical has only become mystical because we have chosen – or been educated – to ignore it and live in only a small part of ourselves.

The unconscious can best be thought of as having three levels; first is the preconscious, which consists of all those things we can call to mind at will; second is the personal unconscious, which is the repository of much of our life history and usually inaccessible except in dreams and psychotherapy; and third is the collective unconscious, which is our common heritage of psychological and spiritual pre-dispositions, and usually entirely outside the range of the conscious mind. In meditation, as we shall see, even these deeper levels may lose their mystery.

MEDITATION 5: **Become Conscious of Your Emotions**

Emotions are what give life its colour, and its many ups and downs. Some of us are in touch with our emotions, aware of how to enjoy or deal with them. Most of us like to enjoy positive emotions such as delight and happiness. But painful emotions such as anger and fear can pose major problems. Others of us are less sure of our emotional lives, and may repress many emotions – even positive ones. Meditation puts us in touch with our emotions and helps us handle them more effectively.

1 *Sit comfortably and turn your attention to how you feel. If your feelings happen to be neutral (though remember that even boredom is a feeling!), bring to mind a situation that caused you anger, fear, frustration, embarrassment or another troublesome emotion.*

2 *Try to identify where the emotion is in the body. In your stomach? In your chest? In your head or your back? Pay attention to the sensation. What words would you use to describe it? Become familiar with the sensation.*

3 *Now gently let it go. Feel the sensation gradually dissolve. If the thought that gave rise to it remains, don't try to push it away, simply distance yourself from it, observe it as if it doesn't belong to you. Allow it to fade.*

The Whole You

These introductory meditations should have helped you feel more integrated as a person, with mind, body and emotions more sensitive toward each other. They should also have helped you to notice that in reality mind, body and emotions constantly influence and affect each other. Anxious or angry thoughts lead to anxious or angry emotions reflected in anxious or angry bodily sensations. Similarly, if the body is tense, it sends tense signals to both mind and emotions. If negative emotions such as anger or fear are aroused, they can be useful in helping us fight injustice or avoid danger. But they can also be counter-productive when experienced out of their proper context – and when the mind and the body both respond unnecessarily. Only when we are conscious of our emotions can we hope to control the potentially hazardous mental and physical effects that they may have.

We usually think of self-consciousness as a form of embarrassment, however, this kind of self-consciousness is simply the self-awareness we have when other people are looking at us – and perhaps thinking us foolish or awkward or inadequate. True self-consciousness implies self-knowledge and self-acceptance. Meditation helps us to move toward self-acceptance. It teaches us to let go of self-judgements. We are who we are, neither greater nor lesser, neither better nor worse.

MEDITATION 6: **Become Conscious of Yourself**

Meditation enables us to recognize how transitory and meaning-less are feelings such as embarrassment. In addition the very act of sitting quietly with ourselves engenders a sense of comfort with who we are, of being at ease and at home with ourselves.

1   *Start this meditation as usual by sitting comfortably, with your back straight. Allow your awareness to run through the body.*

2   *Become conscious of yourself as a presence, as occupying space, as a part – a vital part – of creation. Don't allow this to become egotistical. You are not judging yourself or praising yourself, simply being aware of yourself as alive and therefore of value.*

3   *Be aware of yourself as someone with a life-history. Don't try to recall any of this history or start to think about it. Have a sense instead of your present self as being built upon your past self, as if you are sitting on top of the past years of your life.*

4   *Now be aware of yourself with a future, a future you into which you are continually growing.*

5   *Finally, recognize the self thus has no boundaries, and is limited neither by past nor future, or even by the fluctuating opinions others may have of us.*

Beginning Sitting Meditation

You should by now have an idea of what meditation is about. You know it involves calming the mind by attending to a single stimulus. You know it unifies mind, body and emotions, and helps toward self-knowledge and self-understanding. You know the benefits, mental and physical, that it can bring. Now is the time to build upon this knowledge and upon the preliminary meditations by starting formal sitting meditation practice. Initially, it is a good idea to experiment a little with how best to sit. Without practice, the human body is not comfortable in any one position for very long (one reason we feel the need to move so often), but sitting meditation works best if the body can stay still – and I mean really still except for the breathing – for the allotted period of time, whether this be five minutes or an hour. As we saw earlier, stillness in the body encourages stillness in the mind, hence the need to experiment to find what position feels best.

You will be familiar with pictures of meditators sitting in the lotus position, with back straight, legs crossed and each foot placed upon the opposite thigh. This position is well-nigh impossible for most adults without long practice and suffering. An easier alternative is the so-called perfect position, in which one of the crossed legs is left on the ground, and the foot of the other is lifted to rest on the opposite calf. This position is attainable by most people with practice. Initially, the knees tend to stay up from the floor, but with patience and perseverance (never force the knees down with your hands; use only gentle muscular pressure by the legs themselves) you will be able to lower the knees further.

If you can't manage this position, sit with normal crossed legs. If that's impossible, sit in an upright chair, with the feet flat on the floor. But whichever position you adopt, the back must be straight, and the head upright. This keeps sleep at bay, strengthens the back, and is said in yoga to allow energies to rise up through the spine to the head.

Let's assume you find you can sit comfortably on the floor (to begin with, you'll only be sitting for some five minutes each meditation session). Now make or buy a small hard cushion that lifts your bottom when seated about four inches from the floor. Once on your cushion, fold your left leg (or the other way around if you prefer) and draw the heel in until it is touching the cushion. Slide gently forward until you are almost sitting on this heel, take hold of the right leg and cross it over the left, placing the right foot on the left calf, or leaving it on the floor in front of the calf if this is too difficult. Try to lower your knees as far as possible. Finally, place your hands in your lap, palms upward, the right one resting in the left.

You are almost ready to begin.

A Time and Place to Sit

You now know how to sit for meditation, so when and where should you sit? The golden rule is not to be over-ambitious, or too concerned with long-term goals. Far more people start meditating than keep meditating, and one of the reasons is that they attempt too much too soon – being thrown in at the deep end may work for monks, but not for busy lay-people. So work out what can best fit in with your schedule and your family life. Some three-quarters of meditators prefer morning sessions, most of the rest choose the evening. But you may find some other time of day is best or more convenient for you. Try to keep to your chosen time, so that at the appointed hour the mind turns naturally to meditation.

A quiet place is desirable, even essential to begin with. A special room is best, but few people have that luxury, so choose a corner of a peaceful room or even somewhere outside if you live in a warm climate. As with time, try to keep to your special place. You may like to define your space with something distinctive – a small rug on the floor, or perhaps a shelf with crystals, to help to turn your mind toward your practice. You should not allow small sounds elsewhere in the house to disturb you while sitting, but it is important to avoid intrusive noise. If you're alone in the house disconnect the telephone. Music can be used in meditation, but for the most part, especially for beginners, it's best to sit in silence.

How Long to Sit

Short sessions of steady meditation are better than longer sessions with the mind wandering at will. Start with as little as five minutes. Once the five-minute habit is firmly established you can either decide to increase the time by another five minutes, or allow the session to run on for as long as feels right after the five minutes are up. With the latter method you may find after a few sessions you are sitting for 15 minutes although it still seems like five. However, the former method is safer in that it keeps things organized and leaves you in control.

As your practice develops, aim to build up to 30 minutes a day, either in a single session or in two 15-minute sessions. Eventually, an hour a day is the ideal, but quality remains more important than quantity. Set a quiet timer to tell you when your time is up, and get to your feet slowly and deliberately when you feel ready.

What to Wear

Just as it's best to have a set time and place to meditate, so it's best to keep something special to wear. The keyword is, of course, comfort. Whatever you wear should be loose and comfortable on the body. In cold weather, make sure it will keep you warm enough, particularly as your meditation sessions become longer. In hot weather, choose something cool, but whatever the temperature, natural materials are preferable to man-made. Some people like to shower before sitting, regarding this as both a purifying and a calming ritual, and some like to sit naked, even when outdoors if they have a sheltered corner of the garden. Other people find nudity distracting, and for some people privacy may be difficult to come by. Unless you are practising naked, try to ensure that whatever you wear carries some symbolic significance that will help lead the mind to meditation.

One way to introduce symbolic overtones is through colour. White is regarded in the West as a symbol of purity and transcendence. The saffron and maroon colours favoured by Hindus and some Buddhist groups are said to represent the sun and thus enlightenment, while in the Christian religion purple is the most sacred of all colours, representing God's majesty. Green is a more pagan, earthly colour, while blue stands for tranquility and spaciousness. These meanings are not simply assigned arbitrarily to colours. They represent some of the effects that colours have upon the mind. Choose whatever colour appeals to you, even if you only have the colour in a scarf or some other accessory. Wear the colour each time you sit.

Some shapes also carry special significance. Thus a cloak is a symbol of privacy – when you put it around you it represents withdrawal into meditation. A belt or a rope around the waist is said to symbolize the link between man and the divine. A scarf, such as those given in Tibetan Buddhist ceremonies, symbolizes the act of offering – a giving of oneself to the enlightened mind, which is said to be inside all of us and revealed through meditation. And bare feet represent humility, and the putting aside of earthly things.

Another way of using symbols is through ornaments such as necklaces. Some people choose a necklace of their birth stones. Others opt for simple wooden beads or a pendant with spiritual significance such as a cross or the Sanskrit symbol for *Om*, said to be the primal sound that brought the universe into being. Some ornaments or garments are endowed with well-known religious or spiritual connotations while others may represent a more personal symbolism. But whatever item you choose will help you to focus your attention toward your meditation session. You should reserve your item exclusively for your sitting and change out of your meditation clothes when the session is over.

The Moving World

We have already spoken about the frantic pace of modern life, and the constant distractions with which it presents us. Distractions pull the mind first this way and then that, preventing it from attending properly to any one stimulus or indeed to any one train of thought. In the course of time, meditation trains the mind to such an extent that the meditator can sit tranquilly, undisturbed by even the most frenetic activity. In some traditions, the teacher even deliberately introduces distractions to gauge the progress of his pupils by watching their reactions. One of my Nyingma (the oldest school of Tibetan Buddhism) teachers used to let out a loud shout like a whiplash at unpredictable moments during our session in order to note if any of us flinched. At other times he would clap two boards together with a crack like a pistol shot. (Although my body remained still when this happened, I can't pretend something did not startle deep inside me!).

However, the ability to sit through distractions takes long practise, and in the early stages it is important to learn explicit strategies for dealing with them. Meditation 7 gives you general guidelines on these distractions. Here it is important to say something about the distractions caused by pain or physical discomfort. In the *vipassana* practice of Theravadin Buddhism one is taught to sit through the pain or discomfort. But in the early

MEDITATION 7: **Deal with Distractions**

When dealing with distractions from the environment it is important to refrain from trying to shut the distraction out. Deliberate attempts to remain unmoved by it invariably meet with failure. The following meditations are designed to help you develop the technique of dealing with distractions.

1   *First, allow the distraction to register on your mind, in much the way that you observe your thoughts.*

2   *Next, as with your thoughts, remain an observer rather than a participant in the distraction. Don't allow it to dominate you. If you do, you become part of it.*

3   *Don't try to identify the distraction. If it is a sudden noise from the street, let it remain just a sudden noise from the street, rather than trying to decide whether it's a lawn mower or a power tool, and which neighbour is responsible for causing it.*

4   *Don't respond emotionally to the distraction. Judging it as unpleasant or pleasant, or resenting the fact that your neighbours or your family can be so noisy, only strengthens the chances of the noise distracting you from your meditation. It is simply a noise, nothing more.*

MEDITATION 7: *continued*

5   *You may then find that the distraction fades into the background. As with a pain it is still there, but it no longer bothers you. If it doesn't fade, recognize it nevertheless as a learning experience, of value to your meditation. And if you do succeed in remaining unmoved by it, this is a sign of good progress.*

6   *Finally, don't abandon the meditation session because of a distraction. If you do, the distraction has won. It is sometimes said that you should soften yourself around the distraction, instead of becoming hard to it. Experience will help you recognize what this means.*

stages of meditation practice allow yourself to move slowly if the pain becomes unbearable. Rub the place concerned (I tend to get cramp sometimes in my feet and legs), but try not to break the flow of meditation. Be aware of the movement as you change position, and then of your hand gently massaging the place concerned, but do not become distracted by thoughts about the distraction. When the pain eases, slowly resume your meditation position.

In the case of a constant pain that you are trying to ease by means of meditation, use the pain as a focus for meditation. Observe it steadily and if possible objectively. It is a pain but you are not the pain. The pain is there but it need not disturb you. The Buddhist meditation teacher will tell you that the result of this act of simple observation is that the pain may suddenly become "empty", i.e. become simply something that is happening, but something that has no existence outside your own mind, something that is dependent upon the mind and can be ignored by the mind, something that has no real meaning beyond the meaning you choose to give to it. This may help you to ignore the pain, to attach less importance to it.

This attitude toward pain takes time and patience to achieve. Don't expect to succeed the first time you try. Patience and perseverance, as with all aspects of meditation, are essential. But having focused upon the pain in this way, you can then turn the meditative attention away from it. After this experience of "emptiness", people tend to say things like "The pain is still there, but it doesn't bother me so much".

Meditation develops our concentration, which in turn can improve our powers of recall. We all complain from time to time about our memories, sometimes with the mistaken belief that we remembered things far better in childhood than we do now. But the main reason for memory lapses is that we are so bombarded with information, sensations and experiences that we have no time to take things in. Children's lives, for all their complexities, are rather more straightforward than ours. Not only are there fewer things for them to remember, they often approach the interesting ones with more focus and enthusiasm than we do as adults.

Meditation 8 helps show how the techniques of attention associated with meditation can increasingly become part of everyday life, with obvious advantages for efficiency and effectiveness. We can summarize what these techniques teach us by saying that meditation enables us to absorb the world rather than skate over the surface.

MEDITATION 8: **Become Conscious of Memory Lapses**

The first part of this meditation helps you to recognize how fallible your memory is, both for the events of childhood and for those that are more recent. The second part shows how attention can improve things.

1 *Think back to childhood. You made the journey to and from school thousands of time. How many of these journeys can you recall (the average even in young adults is only about a dozen)? Now try to recall everything you did on this day a week ago.*

2 *For five minutes each day (longer if you wish) carry out a silent running commentary on everything you are doing. Just before bedtime, see how much you can remember of those five minutes compared to any other comparable period during the day.*

Another aid to attention and to memory is to develop the habit of trying to recall. Again, just before bedtime, try to recall all the events of the day from first awakening onward.

Absorbing the World

Buddhism uses meditation to redirect our perception of the world so that rather than being deceived by outward appearances and by our conditioned conceptions of these appearances, we are able to experience reality on a different level. Buddhism describes this absorption of the world as seeing into the true nature of things.

We handicap our ability fully to absorb the world because we make too clear a distinction between ourselves and the rest of creation, as if we end at the envelope of our skin. In fact, at the bodily level, we constantly take in sustenance from the world – air, food, water – and give it back to the world. Moreover, the metals and chemicals that make up our bodies are identical to the metals and chemicals in the outer world. And at the mental level, as already discussed, our impression of the outer world arises only within the mind itself.

Our failure to recognize these facts is responsible for our lack of gratitude to the natural world. This lack of gratitude restricts and diminishes us as people, and leads to our treatment of the environment simply as a resource to be plundered and a dustbin to be filled. Meditation, by helping us dissolve the unnatural boundaries between ourselves and the world, helps us develop this gratitude and realize the sacredness of all creation.

MEDITATION 9: **Become Conscious of the Passing of Time**

We live in a time-haunted world, but "time" is simply a concept invented to try to explain the process of change, or as Buddhism calls it, of impermanence. Nothing remains the same. Meditation helps us see into the true nature of things, and so we must become fully aware of this process of change. One of the best ways of becoming conscious of change is to watch the breath, a meditative technique that we shall use a lot in this book.

- *Place your left hand (right if you are left-handed) on your abdomen. Feel it rise and fall as you breathe. Be aware of this constant coming and going. Each breath, when exhaled, is as irrecoverable as the first moment of creation.*

MEDITATION 10: **Become Conscious of Relaxation**

Tensions creep up on us unawares over the years until they become habitual. Meditation, by allowing us to pay attention to the body, helps us recognize these tensions and let them go. Thanks to this process we then become able to spot and relax new tensions the moment they occur. This practice is intended to help you become aware of tensions and relaxations.

1   *Lie flat on the floor. Tense and relax each group of muscles in turn. Start with the muscles of the calves and thighs. Work upward through the body and then back down the arms to the hands. Hold each tension for a moment before letting it go. Pay particular attention to the back, shoulders and neck.*

2   *Try to stay relaxed after finishing the exercise.*

The Sleeping Self

Meditation helps us awaken from the half-sleep in which we spend much of our waking lives. But it also aids sleep itself. Meditators sleep more easily and peacefully than non-meditators, and often find that meditation helps them to need less sleep. Meditation also gives us greater access to the dream world – by teaching us to pay attention during waking life, meditation helps us to become more aware during sleep. It is said in both Eastern and Western psycho-spiritual traditions that the advanced meditator remains aware not only through dreaming but even non-dreaming sleep (a state akin to profound meditation itself).

An awareness of dreams and an ability to recall them upon waking helps further to dissolve the boundaries between the conscious and the unconscious mind; furthermore the content of dreams may give us insights into the concerns of waking life. In addition, a heightened awareness of dreams facilitates the occurrence of lucid dreams in which the dreamer is aware of dreaming, and can take control of the dream and decide, if not its details, its general direction. Such dreams not only enrich our dream life, but can be used to help solve waking problems. The Nyingma school of Tibetan Buddhism teaches that sleep is a dress-rehearsal for death, and that by gaining control of our dreams we gain control of the process of dying and the transition to the next world.

MEDITATION 11: **Be Conscious of Dreams and Their Meaning**

One of the most effective techniques of dream interpretation is the word association method devised by Carl Jung. The first part of this meditation will help you to recall your dreams and the second part uses this method to help you interpret their meanings.

1 *Put a notebook beside your bed to use as your dream diary. When you wake in the morning lie still for a few minutes and try to recall your last dream. Don't try too hard. Keep the mind open and clear and allow the fragments of your dream to come of themselves. These fragments may prompt the recall of more complete episodes of dreaming. Then write these down, however illogical or foolish they may seem. From time to time during the day try to recall what you have written, and if possible to re-live the flavour of the dream. Recall is also helped if you repeat during the day – and particularly before falling asleep – that you will remember your dreams.*

2 *Select a prominent feature of the dream (an event, a person, a scene, a colour) and write it as a single word in the middle of a sheet of paper. Now in a circle around it, write down each of the associations this symbol brings to mind. Go back to the symbol before each association, rather than setting off on a stream of free associations (with each word leading to the next one). Study your associations. What do they tell you about the symbol and thus the dream?*

Meditation and Spirituality

It is no accident that meditation techniques have primarily developed within the great spiritual traditions. Whether we believe it was through revelation, insight or trial and error, the traditions have been aware for centuries that meditation gives access to profound levels of inner experience recognized as spiritual. The mind stills the intrusive, demanding chatter that often dominates it, and becomes aware of realities that transcend the material world and the space-time continuum, and that are variously described as divine, as the absolute, or as one's own true nature.

However, it is fruitless to meditate with the deliberate intention of accessing these spiritual realities. Whenever you intend that meditation should do something or reveal something, the conscious mind assumes it can do the work for you. Meditation works best if, as soon as you sit on your cushion, all thoughts of goals and attainments are relinquished. You sit in meditation simply because that is what you are doing. In this way no help is requested from the conscious mind.

This is hard for the Western mind to understand. Our education teaches us that we can only achieve by doing, by strength of motivation and fixity of purpose. Meditation teaches us something very different. Self-discipline is certainly needed to remain focused upon the point of attention in meditation. But this is the only kind of discipline required. The meditator concentrates upon the practice of meditation, and whatever arises does so as if by itself. Furthermore, the meditator does not become elated by or attached to whatever arises. The moment elation happens, the conscious mind is back in control, and the experience is lost. It is only when the meditation is over that the meditator ponders what has happened and – if the experience has been sufficiently deep – notices the changes in him or herself that it may have brought about.

What are these changes? They may include an abiding sense of the reality of the spiritual dimension and of the illusory nature of death. They may entail a sense of the interconnectedness of all things, of love as the supreme reality, of a joyful loss of the small, egotistical self we mistakenly believe is who we are. They may involve an increased sense of compassion toward all creation, even a sense that despite the sufferings met with in earthly life, ultimately all things are well and have meaning and purpose.

Does this mean that the committed practice of meditation changes lives on a spiritual as well as a physical and psychological level? For many people yes, but dogmatic answers have no place in meditation. And no prior beliefs – beyond the notion that it is worth a try – should be demanded of those who learn meditation. To summarize the Buddha's teaching on the subject, take nothing on trust. Try the practice and see what happens.

Meditation and Ethical Behaviour

If meditation has a spiritual dimension, is it likely to make us more thoughtful and humane people? Many meditators think so. An increased sense of compassion and an awareness of love as the ultimate reality have been mentioned in the last section as among the changes that may occur in those who become committed meditators. The awareness that arises in meditation both of the interconnectedness of all things and of the fact that each person is not bounded by his or her own skin also leads to a greater sensitivity and commitment to the welfare of other people and of the natural world.

In the great spiritual traditions it is also emphasized that spiritual practice and ethical behaviour are both essential for progress. Both are needed to fulfil one's relationship to the divine and one's relationship to the material world and to everything within it, including animals, plants and the earth itself. Without both, one's development can become one-sided. Spiritual practice without ethical behaviour may lie behind the well-publicized cases of spiritual teachers abusing their pupils, while ethical behaviour without spiritual practice appears incomplete – the individual may for example be ethical toward their family and cultural group but not toward outsiders, ethical toward people but not toward animals, and so on.

MEDITATION 12: **Develop Loving Kindness**

There are certain meditation practices specifically designed to enhance both spiritual and ethical development. We can anticipate one of them here. It is easy to understand (though not always easy to do!), and can be tried out even before we explain specific meditation techniques in Chapters 2, 3 and 4. Known as the *metta* or loving kindness practice in Buddhism, it sits easily with all spiritual beliefs – or with none of them.

1   *Start by calling to mind the person or people or animals or trees you love most in this world. Visualize them if you can, and allow your feelings of love for them to arise strongly. Imagine that you are embracing them and protecting them with this love.*

2   *When this sense is firmly established, widen this circle of love so that, without losing its power, it embraces your close friends and other people or aspects of nature dear to you.*

3   *Repeat this meditation regularly.*

MEDITATION 13: **Extend Your Circle of Love**

When you have firmly established a circle of love that embraces loved ones and friends, you may like to try extending your loving kindness further to include all living things.

1 *Start by repeating Meditation 12. When your circle of love embracing loved ones is firmly established, widen it so that it embraces acquaintances and colleagues.*

2 *Finally widen the circle until it includes the whole of creation, including animals, plants and even the people you may actively dislike.*

You may find that your circle of love can be extended quite readily to your loved ones but becomes difficult with close friends, and impossible beyond that. No matter. Don't make too much effort to extend it, or the practice becomes artificial. Repeat it regularly for family and friends, and then go further when it seems comfortable. It is vital to remember that in this as in all meditation practices, you are not attempting to do all the work consciously. When deeper levels of the mind become aware of what is happening, it is the practice itself that yields results.

chapter 2

Concentration and Mindfulness

We are now ready to begin more formal meditation practice. But don't forget that the meditations learned in Chapter 1 remain helpful and should be practised along with those that follow.

Chapter 1 explained that meditation involves focusing upon a chosen stimulus and remaining centred upon it without becoming lost in mental chatter. It stressed that the focused attention learned in meditation should then be brought into daily life, with attendant advantages for efficiency, effectiveness and the operation of memory. This focused attention in daily life is often referred to as mindfulness, the ability to put one's mind fully into the immediate experience of the present moment.

Mindfulness allows us to relate more fully to experience – to absorb the world, and to see beyond the superficial appearance of things and the conditioned ideas we have about them. You will find in addition that mindfulness adds greatly to the interest of life. By taking proper notice of everything around us we find that everyday things reveal qualities of which we were previously unaware. We may even find that these things take on an unexpected beauty that enhances our experience of them.

Starting and Keeping a Meditation Diary

Having decided when to meditate and what to wear, and having prepared your meditation space, you need one more helpful aid to your practice, a meditation diary. Any notebook will do, but it is generally advisable to treat everything surrounding your meditation as a little special, and therefore to obtain a reasonably substantial hardback book that will hold together over the weeks and months as you consult it as well as add to it.

The diary is not just for recording your experiences during the formal meditation sessions, which we will come to in a moment. Use it for copying down any pieces of information about meditation that you find helpful, and for any passages from relevant books that appeal to or inspire you. These may include poems, pieces from the Bible, the Koran, the Hindu scriptures and the Buddhist *sutras*. Your sense of the value of these pieces and your willingness to re-read them frequently is greatly enhanced if you write legibly. Use whatever colours seem to you to go best with the pieces concerned.

Keeping a record of your experiences in each meditation session is of particular value. It encourages you to keep practising (it is useful, if your practice becomes desultory, to look back at earlier enthusiastic comments – where and why have you lost that enthusiasm?), and enables you to keep track of your progress.

By "progress" I don't mean continual apparent progress. One of the frustrating features of meditation is that "progress" is never an upward curve. A session may seem to go wonderfully well. Your mind remains clear and focused throughout. You have the distinct impression that you have become an effective meditator. Yet the following day your mind hops and jumps about uncontrollably, and you seem to have slipped back several weeks. It is inevitable that meditation should be like this, because our ability to sit with a clear mind depends – sometimes to a major extent – upon what kind of day we have just had or what kind of day lies ahead. And if we can manage to hold the mind steady for even a few seconds on chaotic days, we may have learnt more about meditation than we do from sessions where all seems to go well.

Keep a record in your diary of the context of each session, relating your meditation to the things that happen around you. And try to be as specific as possible about the meditation itself. It is of little use simply to write that you have had a good session. What was "good" about it? If the session appeared to go badly, what was "bad" about it? What kind of thoughts distracted you? Was the problem caused by the fact that the novelty of meditation has worn off and the sitting has become perfunctory and desultory? What can you do to improve things?

You can illustrate your diary if this helps you to clarify your meditative experiences.

The Meaning of Concentration and Mindfulness

You have learnt a great deal about meditation, and now you are going to put this into practice and learn far more through direct experience. You prepare yourself and sit down in your meditation space. You set your timer for five minutes, you close your eyes (open-eyed meditation comes later; to begin with it is better to keep the eyes closed). You decide to concentrate upon your breathing, which we will discuss more fully in the next section, and you begin. But a question immediately arises in your mind. What do we mean by concentration? Memories of being told to concentrate at school come back, together with associated images of grim determination. Is that what is required in meditation.

Decidedly not. In meditation the mind is held steady and focused not by grim determination, but by its own ability to enter into awareness once we stop distracting and bombarding it with an unbroken stream of thinking. So how do you try to stop the stream of thinking? The answer is you don't try. If you want to recognize the impossibility of stopping your thoughts (at least before you become an experienced meditator) try to remain without thoughts for a full minute. Very few people can do so. In meditation, you therefore allow thoughts to arise as they will, but because of your focus upon your breath or upon another chosen stimulus, you no longer pay attention to them. They arise and pass away, like bubbles in a bottle. They can do as they wish, your attention is elsewhere. If you do become distracted for a moment by a thought, you gently let it go and return to your point of focus. You do not become impatient or frustrated with yourself. Frustration and impatience only disturb the mind, and encourage you to give up meditation in despair or anger.

In meditation therefore, the mind remains light rather then heavy, and stays with the point of focus, watching it carefully yet with a certain detachment. The point of focus is there to carry you from the random preoccupations of the mind to a clear space where thoughts may even cease for moments together but where, whether they arise or not, thoughts do not intrude. Once the practice develops, concentration on the point of focus requires less and less effort on your part.

Similarly with mindfulness in daily life. Mindfulness means that the point of focus is now upon whatever one is doing, instead of being lost in thoughts that have little or no connection with it. Thinking, of course, is an essential feature of the mind. The problem lies in disorganized thinking. When thinking is required, mindfulness helps develop the ability to think productively and creatively (creativity flourishes when the mind is open and receptive). In effect, you become mindful of your own thoughts and of what you are trying to achieve by them.

Working With Breath

Once you are on your cushion with your back upright, your legs crossed, your hands linked on your lap and your eyes closed, your meditation begins. Bring your attention to the area between your upper lip and your nose, where the air seems cool as you breathe in and warm as you breathe out, and keep your attention there throughout the meditation session. When thoughts or emotions occur, pay them no attention. They come and go as we have said like bubbles in a bottle, or clouds crossing the sky. They are a separate activity of the mind which does not distract you. For you, the mind is focused on the subtle sensation of the in-breath and the out-breath.

If you can't feel this sensation just below the nose, move your attention to inside the nose, where you can feel it. The exact position is of no consequence. But resist the temptation to follow the breath down into the lungs. Stay focused on the one chosen place. Should you find your attention wandering, bring it gently back to the breathing. It is sometimes said that you should be like a sentry at the gates of a city, who never leaves his post and watches carefully everything that passes in and out of the gates.

There are many reasons why the breath is a good point of focus. Firstly, breathing accompanies us from the cradle to the grave. Without the breath we would die within minutes. Therefore

MEDITATION 14: **Discover the Nature of Your Breathing**

Breathing depends upon the action of the diaphragm – the largest muscle in the body, which is located just below the lungs and above the solar plexus. The solar plexus is, apart from the brain itself, the largest concentration of nervous tissue in the body. Deep breathing – which means breathing from low down rather than taking deep breaths – soothes and calms what is sometimes called the second brain. This meditation helps you to observe exactly how you are breathing and how to correct your breathing.

1   *Sit or lie down, breathe as normal, and watch what is happening. Are you breathing from the top of the chest, or from deep down in the abdomen?*

2   *Focus upon the diaphragm, and try and draw the breath down to the base of the lungs. The lungs can expand far more here than they can imprisoned behind the ribs higher up.*

3   *Now switch attention to the texture of your breathing. Is it gentle and rhythmic or snatched and jerky? Is it silent or noisy? Would you describe it as soft or harsh, regular or irregular?*

4   *Once you have identified the faults in your breathing, spend a few minutes correcting them, working upon each in turn.*

it is the gift upon which our lives most depend. Secondly, because of its subtle, transparent quality, the breath is a perfect symbol of the unseen, spiritual world. Thirdly, the breath unifies mind and body – being seemingly non-material like the mind, yet sustaining moment by moment the life of the body. Fourthly, the breath represents our absorption of the outer world, and therefore the unity between outer and inner. Fifthly, by calming our breathing we calm both mind and body.

Watching the breath in this way was the method taught by the Buddha, the prince of meditators. It is the bedrock of all meditation practices. If you use only one practice, this is the one to choose. Even when using some of the other practices explained later in the book it is always good to start each session by focusing upon the breathing for a few minutes before you move on.

If you prefer you can focus upon the gentle rise and fall of the abdomen with each breath rather than upon the point of entry and exit at the nostrils. Experiment with both places if you wish, but don't change between them during a session. And once you find which of them you prefer, it's best to keep to that method. There's a great temptation in meditation to imagine that there is always a better technique than the one you are actually using. Avoid the temptation. Consistency is one of the essentials of good meditation practice.

MEDITATION 15: **Become Mindful of Breathing**

Having identified and corrected the bad habits in your breathing, try to practise good habits during the day.

- *Notice what happens to your breathing if you become anxious, excited or angry. Does the breathing become rapid and shallow at such times? Make a conscious effort to slow it down and draw it deeper into the body.*

- *Notice the effect upon the breathing of certain activities. What happens when you drink coffee or alcohol? If you are a smoker, what happens when you inhale? What happens when you relax? How long does your breathing take to return to normal after exertion?*

- *Try to become more mindful of your breathing. Develop gratitude and respect for the air you breathe and for the body that carries out the breathing.*

MEDITATION 16: **Talk and Breathe**

Notice particularly the relationship between talking and breathing. The two activities are closely connected, because we talk on the out-breath.

1   *Notice that people who talk rapidly and jerkily breathe rapidly and jerkily. People who talk fluently breathe fluently.*

2   *Notice also what happens when you are interrupted in the middle of a sentence. Do you hold your breath for a moment after you've checked the flow of words? Holding the breath in this way is a major cause of the tensions that often build up when we're involved in conversations, particularly in stressful ones or when several people are trying to talk at once.*

3   *Make a conscious effort to relax the breathing during conversations, and specifically to avoid the habit of checking and holding the breath. Nothing should interfere with smooth, regular breathing.*

MEDITATION 17: **Breathe for Health**

Apart from correcting bad breathing habits, you should not try to change your pattern of breathing – as for example in certain yoga exercises – without medical advice and the help of qualified teachers. However, so-called north-south breathing is safe, and very effective for clearing the sinuses and helping ward off respiratory infections.

- *Close one nostril with the thumb, and breathe in normally through the other. Now release the closed nostril and breathe out through it while closing the other with the middle finger. Next breathe in through the open nostril, close it and release and breathe through the other one.*

- *If need be, this practice can sometimes be used during a full meditation session.*

Breath Visualization

The breath can be used in conjunction with visualization to help relax the body and assist healing in meditation. In all the great spiritual and mystery traditions, the ability to visualize is regarded as an important aid to spiritual progress. More recently, sports psychologists have discovered that people generally perform better if they are able to visualize their success in advance (for example, hitting the perfect golf shot, winning the race or executing the perfect dive). Visualization appears to help program both mind and body to achieve the desired outcome.

The easiest way to use visualization in conjunction with breathing is to imagine energizing and healing white light streaming in through the nostrils on the in-breath, and to imagine the darkness of tiredness, tensions and strains streaming out of the nostrils on the out-breath. If there is a specific affliction in the body, the white light can be visualized as flowing through the body to the area concerned, while the cause of the affliction exits on the out-breath. This practice should be used in addition to and not instead of the normal meditation session, during which the attention remains focused upon one point. The two forms of meditation serve different purposes, although the powers of attention developed in normal meditation are an important aid in the use of healing meditation.

MEDITATION 18: **Visualize the Breath with Colours and** *Chakras*

In addition to your normal meditation session, try this meditation which involves visualizing a number of different colours. Although we don't yet know why colour has such an important effect upon the mind and possibly the body, the effect certainly exists. This meditation uses *chakras*, which are non-physical energy complexes said to be centred upon various parts of the body. Each *chakra* is associated with a particular colour. As with colour, we don't know why activation of these *chakras* produces feelings of wellbeing, but we know the effect exists. Provided the benefits are felt, the reasons for them are less important.

- *Begin by visualizing the colour red (visualization is helped by imagining an object of that colour, in this case perhaps a red rose) entering the body on the in-breath and flowing to the base* chakra *located at the perineum (the area just behind the genitals). When this visualization is well-established (say after three breaths), imagine orange flowing to the sacral* chakra *just below the navel. Next, visualize yellow entering the solar plexus* chakra, *followed by green flowing to the heart* chakra, *blue to the throat* chakra, *indigo to the brow* chakra, *and violet to the crown* chakra *at the top of the head.*

- *At the end of the meditation, think of the whole body as energized and purified by these colours.*

Circular Breathing

Until you are able steadily to watch the breath at the nostrils (see p.58) for some 15 minutes each session, it is not advisable to embark upon any other meditation practice. In the practices described in Meditation 18, it is in fact possible to visualize the breath being drawn into the body not through the nose but through the perineum. This form of visualized breathing, without the involvement of colours and *chakras*, is known as circular breathing and is another illustration of our ability, mentioned earlier, to move the consciousness around the body.

Circular breathing is a highly regarded practice both in Hindu and some Buddhist traditions. The practice has two major benefits. Firstly, it demands rather more concentration (which paradoxically some people find makes meditation easier) and thus can deepen meditative abilities, and secondly, it is said to facilitate the movement of energy up through the body to the head, helping the meditator to sit rock steady, and to transmute physical force into spiritual force. Acceptance or rejection of the existence of this second benefit depends upon your belief system, but in all the Eastern and yogic traditions it is taught that bodily energies can follow the path of visualization. We know that the mind can affect the body, and the belief here is that it can do so in subtle ways as yet undetected by science.

MEDITATION 19: **Practise Circular Breathing**

Circular breathing is an alternative breath visualization exercise.

1   *Start by watching the breath at the nostrils as usual. Then after
    12 breaths, imagine the breath is being drawn upward through
    the body, starting at the perineum. By the time the in-breath is
    complete, it has been drawn up as far as the nostrils.*

2   *The out-breath is through the nostrils as usual, but the breath now
    flows in front of and outside the body until it reaches the perineum,
    where it is drawn into the body once more.*

3   *Continue this cycle throughout the meditation. As the breath flows
    down outside the body it becomes re-energized, and draws this
    energy back into the body.*

After working with this practice for some time, many people say
they feel the perineum cool as the air re-enters the body.

In "heel breathing", each breath is thought of as a new breath
which enters through the heels and flows upward through the
entire body and out through the crown of the head. This practice
is used in addition to the normal session, and is best done lying
full length, with the back on the floor.

Focusing on Objects

Although you kept your eyes closed during work with the breath, it is important to be able to meditate with eyes open as well. This ensures that the practice of meditation does not serve to isolate you from the outside world. Meditation is neither an introverted nor an extroverted activity. It is intended neither to turn you too deeply inward nor to direct your attention exclusively outward. Its purpose is to help you to remain balanced and stable in all situations, to attend to whatever is taking place whether inside or outside your head, and eventually to turn effortlessly from one activity to another, always abiding fully in the present.

You can practise your usual breathing meditation with eyes open if you wish (or you can do so sometimes with eyes open and sometimes with eyes closed). When your eyes are open, keep the eyelids half-closed, and the eyes in relaxed semi-focus on the space in front of you. But you can also practise by focusing attention upon an object placed at eye-level in front of you, rather than upon the breathing. If you do so, the choice of object is up to you. Later, when we describe direct contemplation exercises, you may wish to choose a natural rather than man-made object, but this is not necessary at present.

The object not only serves as a point of focus, it helps develop

MEDITATION 20: **Meditate on an Object**

Choose an object that is very familiar to you for this meditation, something you see every day yet take for granted. A tea cup is a good choice; so is a chair or a shoe. Place the object so that it can be viewed comfortably from where you will be sitting.

1 *Sit as usual in meditation and focus on the breathing, keeping your eyes closed. When you feel stabilized, open your eyes and blink several times in rapid succession. Notice the contrast between the moment of darkness with the eyes closed and the miracle of vision when the eyes are open. Turn your attention from your breathing to the object in front of you and look at it steadily, yet without strain. Lower the eyelids slightly, and now blink as little as possible.*

2 *Pay no attention to any thoughts about the object that arise. Pay no attention to any feelings you have about it. Ignore what you know of it. Ignore its function. Make no judgements on its qualities. See it simply as something occupying space. Take in its contours, the light and shadows on its surfaces, the colours, the angles, the texture. See the object as if for the very first time.*

3 *Notice that during this meditation your eyes have an impulse to scan the object and/or to alter their length of focus. Try to resist the temptation to do either of these things. Gaze steadily ahead.*

your ability to see the world. In each moment of waking life we are surrounded by objects, some of them natural, most of them man-made. Yet how much attention do we pay to them? How much do we really know about them? How much do we really know of their shape and their colour, and their appearance from all angles? If we close our eyes can we clearly visualize them? If we were asked to do so, could we draw them accurately from memory? Would we be able to identify them correctly if they were mixed up with several similar objects? The object you may decide to look at in this meditation may be one of the most familiar things in your home, yet perhaps this is the first time you have really seen it, really absorbed it fully into your mind.

As an alternative to using an object, you can simply practise open-eyed meditation by gazing at the wall. This is a method favoured in the Soto school of Zen Buddhism, where the monks sit around the periphery of the meditation hall, each gazing silently and seemingly unblinkingly at a chosen place on the wall in front. If you use this practice, make sure you choose a blank wall. A highly patterned wallpaper or a wall with pictures will be too distracting. Don't allow yourself to start seeing "pictures" in the texture of the wall. The wall must be seen as it is, unembroidered by our own imagination or by concepts about walls.

MEDITATION 21: **Meditate on Form and Space**

The outer world is made up of space as well as form. But we tend to think almost exclusively of the latter, and virtually disregard the former. Yet the one encloses and defines the other. This meditation is a good way of recognizing this, and thus of helping develop the sense of unity and interconnectedness of all things that arises from meditation. You will need a cup for this meditation – perhaps the one you may have used in Meditation 20.

1   *Take the cup in your hand and look at it from all angles. Now think of it as surrounded by empty space, and containing empty space within it. Which is more important for the cup to function as a cup, the space in and around it or the form of which it is composed? Would it be a cup without either the space or the form?*

2   *Look around your room. What makes it a room, the walls or the space they enclose? Which is more important? Look outside. Every object is bounded by space. Would an object exist as itself if it were not for the space around it?*

Artists are often taught to draw the spaces surrounding objects, not the objects themselves. This frees them from concepts about how the objects should look. When the spaces are complete, the objects are seen, as if miraculously, to have been drawn as well.

Focusing on Bodily Movement

Sitting meditation is a static practice, and although much of what is learnt while sitting on your cushion carries over into daily life, it may still happen that once the body starts moving some of the old physical and psychological tensions return, together with the old tendency to be easily distracted.

Partly to help cope with this, a number of moving meditations have been developed. The best known of these is the ancient art of *tai chi chuan*, an excellent practice in its own right, that develops balance and coordination and is said to lead to good health and inner harmony. Practices such as *tai chi chuan* take many years to master, and necessitate the presence of a good teacher, but there are simpler methods of helping you bring greater mindfulness and body awareness into everything you do.

Meditation 2 (see p.21) drew your attention to ways of becoming more conscious of how you move, and this awareness can now be extended by learning the practice of *kinhin*. Meditations 22 and 23 give the practical details, but the principle behind *kinhin* is that one walks very slowly, taking very short steps, and with the attention focused upon each sensation as the steps are taken. The hands are usually held in front and against the body. A fist is made with the left hand, palm toward the ground, and the right hand is closed over the fist and used to press it tightly

MEDITATION 22: **Concentrate on the Lower Body in *Kinhin***

For *kinhin*, select a straight path that allows at least 12 very short paces before you turn around. Hold you hands as described in the text opposite.

1 *Walk forward very slowly by placing the front foot so that the heel comes down level with the opposite toes. Be conscious of each sensation in your legs and lower body. Feel the weight shift from one foot to the other.*

2 *Take your next step at the same slow speed, again placing the front foot so that the heel is level with the toes of the rear foot. Feel each sensation in the legs and lower body.*

3 *Continue for about 12 paces. Then equally slowly and mindfully turn and retrace your steps. Continue the practice for 48 paces, or longer if you wish.*

(but not painfully) into the abdomen just below the navel.

Kinhin sounds easy enough, but in reality most of us walk so badly that it is surprisingly difficult to do well. The feet must move almost in slow motion, and this raises immediate problems with balance, particularly if the ground is a little uneven. The body feels strangely awkward, and the mind responds to this with annoyance and impatience, disturbing any equanimity we may have been feeling. It is only after a little practice in *kinhin* that we recognize how effective it is in re-educating the body, and encouraging the mind to develop more body awareness.

Kinhin can only be practised for a few minutes a day, but there is an important practice you can do while moving normally. Watch the body as much as you can during the course of the day. Apart from writing with your dominant hand, do you habitually favour one side of the body over the other? For example, if you are right-handed do you always step off on your right foot when you start walking and when you climb stairs? Do you open doors with your right hand, pick things up with your right hand, hold a cup in your right hand, operate the television remote control with your right hand? If so, try increasingly to favour the other side, with a view eventually to using both sides equally, and bringing the body back into balance.

Be alert to other ways in which you use the body unevenly, putting undue strain on some muscles and underusing others.

MEDITATION 23: **Concentrate on the Upper Body in *Kinhin***

Next time you practise *kinhin*, concentrate upon the upper body as you walk. Hold your hands as described in the text on p.72.

1 *Check that your hands are pressed against your body without tensing the arms, shoulders or neck muscles.*

2 *Check that the upper body is upright but relaxed, the eyes looking at the ground just ahead.*

3 *Identify why you may have problems with balance.*

4 *Check that your mind is open and clear. Are you trying too hard to stay relaxed and balanced, instead of allowing the body to do the work? If you are finding unexpected problems with this meditation, does this make you impatient with yourself? If so, why is this?*

5 *The next time you try* kinhin, *try to be aware of the whole body. Is it working in harmony?*

Zen meditation teachers often teach *kinhin* in conjunction with very fast walking, alternating the two practices on their word of command, so that the student has to strive to remain mindful while switching unpredictably between very fast and very slow walking. You may wish to try this for yourself.

MEDITATION 24: **Meditate on Movement**

In addition to meditating on bodily movement, it is of value to meditate from time to time on movement outside the body. Some Zen teachers instruct their students to meditate by waterfalls or flowing streams, the aim being both to avoid slipping into a light trance and to recognize the ever-changing nature of reality. Try to take an opportunity to meditate by running water in this way.

- *Allow the eyes and the head to remain still, and the mind to stay in one place rather than to become either mildly hypnotized by the movement or carried along with it. Everything changes, except the eternal presence of the mind.*

- *In the absence of an opportunity to sit by running water, you can try to imagine a running stream or river which has something of the same effect, and also helps develop powers of visualization. Or you can imagine you are standing on a bridge watching a succession of horsemen (or cyclists) pass by below you. Take in the form and colour and other details of each rider, but do not allow your eyes to follow any of them.*

The Tense Self

As your ability to focus in meditation develops, it is valuable to identify not only where the body is tense, but why tensions arise and have arisen. Many of our bodily tensions are directly related to past or present experiences. Some people, with the help of the increased body awareness that comes with meditation, notice that their jaws clench when in a stressful situation. Others notice tension in the back of the head or around the temples. Some find that they hunch their shoulders, some that they tighten their stomach muscles. For others, the tensions seem more internal: they notice tightness in the chest, a raised heart-rate, a sinking in the pit of the stomach, or dryness in the mouth.

Most psychologists are agreed that much of who and what we are is formed in the early years of our childhood. Some psychotherapists consider that many tensions are directly related to traumas and other painful experiences in the past, and that when the tensions are relaxed, memories of these experiences, apparently long forgotten, surface and assist the healing process. We can identify ways in which each of these physical tensions may be associated with a defensive reaction or a reaction of panic or anger going back to childhood. Such reactions are inappropriate in the present, and account for many of the headaches, upset stomachs, or aches and pains with which some of us end the day.

MEDITATION 25: **Identify the Causes of Tensions**

Uncovering some early memories can be painful, and should only be attempted with the help of a qualified psychotherapist. This meditation is designed to locate possible causes of bodily tension rather than reveal anything painful, and involves only handwriting. You will need a pen and some paper.

1   *Write a few sentences on any subject. Study your handwriting. Do you see signs of tension in the way you form words – for example undue pressure on the page, jagged and spiky letters? Are there signs of undue hurry, such as partially formed letters?*

2   *How did you hold the pen? Were you gripping it too tightly? Did you feel comfortable with it, or impatient or even hostile? How did you feel when asked to write something? Enthusiastic or reluctant?*

3   *Now think back to your schooldays. Can you remember anything that may account for the way you write now?*

4   *If you identified problems with your writing and the possible reasons for them, close your eyes and in a meditative state imagine letting all these things go. There is no need to continue carrying them.*

5   *Now write a few more words, relaxing with the pen. Do you notice a difference?*

Meditation and Contemplation

There is often some confusion in people's minds over the difference between meditation and contemplation. There are many similarities between them but also some important differences, not only in practice but in purpose.

The ability to meditate is an aid to contemplation. In both meditation and contemplation the mind is in an open state, acting as an observer. Like meditation, contemplation does not involve attempts by the conscious mind to take control of the processes of thought. Sitting in contemplation, the conscious mind stands back and allows deeper, creative processes to take over. The major difference is that contemplation is a more active process than meditation. One may follow a predetermined train of thought or explore and examine an idea or a set of concepts, or focus upon a meaningful symbol. Unlike meditation, in which the meditator does not attend to the thoughts that arise, contemplation allows such thoughts to be recognized as insights that illuminate the subject that is being contemplated.

One of the finest manuals of contemplation for the Christian is Saint Ignatius Loyola's *The Spiritual Exercises*, which are an important part of the training of Jesuits. In the *Exercises* the student is, for example, instructed to contemplate Christ's Nativity, visualizing each of the people present, and putting himself in the scene as "an impoverished attendant". He "listens" to what is being said and "sees" what people are doing, and contemplates the suffering that Christ will endure during his life on Earth. Though there are no exact parallels to the *Exercises* in the other major traditions, contemplation plays a major part in tantric practices in both Hinduism and Buddhism.

The object of the contemplation in *The Spiritual Exercises* is to experience, at a deep level, the qualities and concerns of those present at the Nativity. The scene is set, the student is inside the scene, and insights into it arise from the unconscious or from an outside spiritual source. Contemplation of this kind requires marked meditative ability, together with powers of visualization. Not surprisingly, it is said that completion of *The Spiritual Exercises*, which should only be attempted with the guidance of a qualified spiritual director, leads to profound spiritual changes.

A less complicated approach for the Christian would be to contemplate the cross, remaining open to the insights and associations that come into awareness. The Hindu might contemplate the symbol for *Om*, the primal sound. A Taoist might use the Tai Chi (the Yin Yang) symbol. A Buddhist might contemplate the Wheel of Life depicting the various levels of existence. A Moslem might use the Arabic script for Allah is Great. The Jew might contemplate the *menorah*, the seven-branched candlestick that indicates the presence of the divine.

The Practice of Contemplation

Contemplation is a state that the meditator can enter at will, not only during sitting practice, but at any time when problem-solving is required. Problems are often solved by sudden insights from the unconscious, rather than by systematic work at the conscious level. Psychologists are unsure of the actual processes involved, but it seems that, once the existence of a problem is recognized, the unconscious gets to work, mentally trying out a variety of solutions until one looks appropriate, which is then pushed up into consciousness. The same appears to be true of creative insights. The conscious mind recognizes a useful idea for the branch of the arts involved, and there follows a period of incubation at the unconscious level before ways of putting the idea into practice illuminate consciousness. Illumination of this kind also seems to operate in the sciences, which make as much use of creative insights as do the arts. Meditation, which quietens the conscious mind and allows more access to the unconscious, materially helps this process. Contemplation takes matters a little further, since now the mind is presented with a "seed" upon which to work.

When using contemplation for problem-solving in daily life, no particular attempt is made to decide in advance what kind of solution is likely to be acceptable. The mind simply holds the

MEDITATION 26: **Contemplate a Symbol**

One of the best ways to practise contemplation is with the use of a symbol. An excellent one to choose is the so-called Celtic Cross, which is a cross on which a circle is superimposed, its centre on the point at which the arms of the cross meet the upright, and its circumference inside the four points of the cross. The Celtic Cross is used in some Christian groups, but it seems to have originated well before Christianity, which suggests that it has universal significance. Carl Jung stressed that symbols, as opposed to logos and trademarks (which originate in the conscious mind), arise spontaneously from the universal, collective unconscious. As such, they provide keys back into the unconscious.

1   *Paint or draw the Celtic Cross on a sheet of paper and mount it at eye-level. Settle in meditation and focus on the breathing to centre yourself. When you feel ready, open your eyes, as in Meditation 20 (see p.69), and look steadily at the cross, with your mind open. If thoughts unconnected with the symbol occur, disregard them.*

2   *Remain like this throughout the contemplation. Don't deliberately think about the symbol or try to "interpret" it. Just contemplate it.*

3   *After a time insights may start to arise. For this meditation, you should look at these mentally to secure them in the memory.*

problem in awareness – actually looking at it if it involves concrete issues – and allows solutions to emerge. Should they fail to do so, the mind leaves the problem to the unconscious, and turns to other things. The very fact of having contemplated the problem starts the process toward a solution or a resolution, which in fact may not emerge into consciousness until days, weeks or even months – sometimes perhaps years – later.

It is clear that we use only a very small part of the potential of the mind. Quite why this should be, when we have clearly evolved such extraordinary mental powers, is unclear. But there is no doubt that meditation and contemplation help give us access to more of these mental powers. Gurdjieff, a sage of modern times, put it that we each live in a beautiful house, yet most of us never move out of the basement. Carl Jung used a similar metaphor. It is not surprising that teachers such as Gurdjieff and Jung, together with mystics and spiritual teachers of all ages, constantly admonish us to awake. The alternative is to go through life half-asleep, virtual strangers even to ourselves.

Like meditation, contemplation involves a certain lightness of mind. Instead of grim determination, the mind is allowed to enter an expectant watchful state, while at the same time not knowing what it is that one expects, but recognizing it when it enters one's awareness.

Visualization in Tantric Buddhism

In Tibetan Buddhism, the tantras involve using intense visualizations to develop qualities said to be latent in all beings – compassion, wisdom, and ultimately the enlightened mind. My first experience of tantra came after meeting a Tibetan lama. We talked together in his still, quiet room for an hour, never mentioning practice. That evening in meditation, to my surprise I became intensely aware of someone sitting opposite me. With my eyes closed, how could I be aware in this way? I can only say that I was. As the meditation drew to a close, this presence rose above my head, descended through my crown, and came to rest in my heart. The experience seemed objective and remarkable. I later mentioned it to pupils of the lama, who informed me I had experienced the lama's own practice, known as guru yoga. I had somehow absorbed this practice just by being in his presence.

Western science has no explanation for experiences of this kind, although Eastern psycho-spiritual traditions accept them as a matter of course. Tibetan Buddhism would not necessarily recognize the distinction between inner and outer experience, but on this occasion my practice spontaneously turned from an internal meditative focus to an external contemplative one. One should never strive for, or try to cling to, experiences of this kind, as this will inhibit the very processes that give rise to them.

MEDITATION 27: **Tantric Contemplation**

1 *For beginners, this contemplative practice is best done with eyes closed. Sit in meditation, centre yourself by focusing on the breathing, then imagine that sitting facing you is a revered figure (a saint or bodhisattva, the Buddha or Christ, a Hindu deity, or an historical person whose qualities you admire). Build up the visualization with as much detail as possible.*

2 *Now see the visualization radiating the qualities you would like in yourself – love, wisdom etc. Spend the whole meditation contemplating this figure and these radiations.*

3 *At the close of the meditation, visualize the figure rising above your head, then bringing all these qualities down into your heart.*

It does not matter whether you consider that this practice is simply a way of further developing qualities that are already within you, or whether you feel that in some way you are obtaining help from outside yourself. The important thing is that the practice is a highly effective one for personal/spiritual growth. Some teachers stress that one should in any case forget the distinction between inner and outer, and realize instead that all things are interconnected.

Compassionate Contemplation

Of all the qualities that can be aroused through contemplation, compassion is one of the most important. We looked in Chapter 1 at loving kindness meditation (see Meditations 12 and 13; pp.50 and 51), which involves extending to one's friends the feelings of love that one has for those near and dear, and then progressively extending these feelings to acquaintances and colleagues, including those one may dislike, and eventually to the whole world. Compassionate contemplation produces a similar effect, and is particularly valuable in that it can be focused effectively upon animals and plants. Compassion should embrace all sentient beings, and even the physical environment. It has always suited the human race to suppose that animals and plants are inferior to us, because this belief allows us to exploit them as we please. A similar supposition is extended to the environment, which we can then assume we can "develop" and plunder indiscriminately. In reality, we share the world with animals and plants and depend on them for our very existence – and depend also upon the Earth, which provides the raw materials that sustain humans, animals and plants alike.

The practice of meditation in itself typically leads to a growth in compassion, because it allows us to be in harmony firstly with ourselves and then, by extension, with the rest of creation. In

MEDITATION 28: **Contemplate the Suffering of Animals**

In this meditation, it is the fact of suffering rather than its cause or remedy that is to be contemplated, and specifically the suffering of our fellow sentient beings, animals and plants.

1 *Focus upon animals, either a particular species, or the idea of animals in general. Initially, make no attempt to call to mind anything specific about them. Just think of the animals concerned, and see what mental pictures arise.*

2 *Once these visualizations are established, allow insights into the qualities of animals to arise.*

3 *Now contemplate their sufferings, the many species now extinct, the suffering of farm animals, the suffering of animals killed for sport, of animals bred for their fur, of animals used in experiments. Contemplate also the suffering of animals caused by the loss of their natural habitat.*

4 *Finish the meditation by embracing all animals with compassion. See them as receiving this compassion, and the compassion easing their suffering.*

5 *Notice how the meditation has increased your awareness of how we humans exploit animals.*

addition, the meditator sees increasingly through the shallow egotistical construction that we mistakenly assume is who we are, and in consequence sensitivity, thoughtfulness and compassion naturally develop in place of greed and selfishness.

An increased awareness of the suffering within creation is associated with this compassion. All the great spiritual traditions deal with the problem of suffering. Even though it is seen as part of the learning experience that is life on Earth, the traditions nevertheless teach ways of overcoming suffering. These may involve faith in a higher power, or avoidance of the three pitfalls of ignorance (failure to develop a true understanding of existence), greed (the desire to possess and hold on to things for ourselves) and aversion (the desire to avoid, punish or destroy the things we dislike or the people who oppose us). Meditations 28 and 29 give details of how some of the emotions associated with compassion can be further developed through contemplation. The meditations essentially help us to recognize the suffering of animals and plants, largely caused by the way in which they are treated by our fellow men and women.

MEDITATION 29: **Contemplate the Suffering of Plants**

It may seem strange to think of plants as suffering. We assume they have no feelings because they lack a central nervous system. Yet, central nervous system or not, plants are in many ways far more intelligent (i.e. effective at solving problems) than we are. They register the existence of problems (for example drought, insect attack, restricted space) and develop intelligent ways of counteracting them, thus ensuring their survival.

1 *Contemplate the plant world, from small grasses to tall trees. Allow insights into our dependence upon them to arise, together with gratitude to them. Life on Earth depends on plants.*

2 *Contemplate the way we exploit plants, the many species lost every day, the destruction of the rain forests.*

3 *Allow regret for our treatment of plants to arise, together with compassion for their sufferings.*

MEDITATION 30: **Contemplate Happiness**

Happiness – wellbeing – is something for which we all long. Yet for many of us it remains elusive.

1 *Contemplate the feeling of happiness. Allow insights to arise on how it feels to be happy, and on how fleeting the feeling often is.*

2 *Allow insights to arise into the causes of happiness and the causes of unhappiness.*

3 *Allow insights to arise into the happiness and unhappiness you may be causing to others, whether human, animal or plant. What is the reason for your behaviour?*

4 *How can unhappiness be transformed into happiness?*

Meditations 28–30 are not intended to arouse guilt, but to help insights of clarity and understanding to arise, and perhaps a determination toward action. But as with all contemplation, it is neither possible nor desirable to specify objectives and outcomes in advance. Contemplation is simply an openness to the qualities that are already there inside oneself.

Moving into Mindfulness

The practice of mindfulness was touched upon in Chapter 1, with the description of maintaining a mental commentary for a set time upon each of our actions (see Meditation 8; p.41). The aim of the meditation was to keep the mind in the present moment, and this is exactly what is meant by mindfulness. Most of the time our minds are concerned with anything but what we are doing and experiencing in this moment. Notice how, although you may make the same journey to work or to the shops virtually every day of the week, you may be unable to recall the names of the streets you pass, or the names above the shops, or the colours of the houses. Notice how it is frequently difficult to draw, on demand, many of the most familiar objects we use during the day – our own car, the clutter on our desk, the pictures on the wall.

Why is mindfulness, the ability to stay in the present and take note of what we are doing, so important? The obvious practical advantage is that it assists memory. How often during the day do we search unavailingly for the object we had in our hands just a moment ago, or for the place where we put our spectacles or our car keys? How often do we read a page in a book, yet when we turn over recall little of what it is we have read? And how often do we remember our dreams, even though research suggests we each of us dream for a total of some two hours every night?

But there is more to mindfulness than this. Mindfulness allows us to appreciate the texture of experience in a way impossible if our minds are in some place other than where we happen to be. Without mindfulness we miss so much in life. Without mindfulness we become restless, bored and dissatisfied, forever seeking some new sensation other than the one offered to us. Without mindfulness we miss so much of the beauty and the poetry in life, the fascination of experiencing this mysterious business of being ourselves.

Meditation is mindfulness. Mindfulness of breathing, or of whatever stimulus we have chosen to use as our point of focus. Contemplation is mindfulness. Mindfulness of whatever it is we are holding in the forefront of awareness. Life itself should be mindfulness, mindfulness of each passing moment and of the gifts that it brings. Too often we hardly notice these gifts because, instead of absorbing them, we dismiss them as of little relevance to our interests or concerns.

Once we have embarked upon the path of meditation, mindfulness in daily life can come naturally. By learning to focus the mind when we are sitting on our cushion, we develop the habit of paying more attention to experiences when we are not sitting. The following meditations help expand further this sense of mindfulness and of the present moment.

Mindfulness of Actions and Behaviour

The very act of meditation – opening oneself to one's own essential being – leads naturally to ethical behaviour, and helps one to behave with sensitivity and compassion to other beings in daily life. Mindfulness helps this process. Too often we are so bound up in ourselves that we are not conscious of the needs and the problems of others. We are deaf and blind to the signals that suggest someone needs our help, or that we have unwittingly wounded someone with our words or our deeds.

Mindfulness means focusing not just upon what we are seeing, hearing and doing. It means mindfulness of these signals and of the effects our behaviour has upon humans, animals, plants and the environment. Mindfulness thus can be a tall order. It would be an even taller one if we had to do it consciously all the time. But as mindfulness develops, much of this ethical behaviour arises naturally. Christmas Humphreys, one of the people responsible for bringing Buddhism to the West in the last century, gives the example of seeing someone drop an umbrella in the street, and of bending down to pick it up and returning it to them, without premeditation and without holding on to the act of kindness in order to polish our ego. Acts of this kind arise naturally and spontaneously from mindfulness. Mindfulness recognizes that there is something of value that needs to be done, and prompts us to do it.

MEDITATION 31: **Be Mindful of Eating**

At first sight, some of these mindfulness meditations may appear rather dull. But this is only because we have learned the way of unmindfulness, and imagine that excitement is only to be found in novelty. The habit of unmindfulness prevents us from recognizing that each moment of life is novel. Each moment is a new beginning, a new experience, a visit to somewhere we have never been before. Eating is a good example. We eat every day, yet usually it is only when we have a special treat that we are truly conscious of what we are eating. Usually, while we eat we are too busy talking or thinking or reading the newspaper or watching the television to notice what we are putting into our mouths.

1   *At the next meal, focus just upon the act of eating. Try if possible to take the meal in silence, and without other distractions.*

2   *Eat slowly, putting your awareness in the colour and the texture of the food, in the choices you make of what to eat next, and in the taste and the texture of the food when it is in your mouth.*

3   *Be mindful of the act of swallowing. Feel gratitude for the earth and the plants that have provided this food, for the many people, from the farmer to the cook, who have helped bring it to your table.*

The great traditions teach us that we should be mindful of what is going on in our heads at all times. Much of our thinking is wasteful, and concerned with our own wants and fantasies. The traditions tell us also to be mindful of our speech – not by watching every word, but by not wasting time in idle chatter, and in particular by refraining from saying negative things about others or spreading gossip. In the end, such gossip not only harms others, but demeans ourselves.

We cannot, of course, plunge immediately into this kind of mindfulness. Much of it develops, little by little, as a result of our meditation practice. But we can decide in advance to be mindful of a particular area of our lives – whether it is the walk to work or the things we say over coffee to our colleagues. Once we start working on this area, other areas tend to open up of their own accord. Once we begin to be aware of the effect that we have in the world, so our horizons broaden and our awareness grows.

Again, this is not a recipe for guilt. Guilt is a self-destructive process that does no good to anyone. It is a recipe for enhanced awareness, for personal growth, for a more effective and more useful (to use the existential term) being-in-the-world.

Start where you can, and go on from there.

Mindfulness When Travelling

We have said a great deal already about awareness while walking; we can now say something about mindfulness during other ways of travelling. I am always surprised when flying how few of my fellow passengers look out of the window. Most of the time they are talking, dozing, reading or watching the in-flight movie. Similarly, when I travel by train I am amazed how few people seem to take any interest in the passing scenery. Many of them are far too interested in the music on their headphones, or in their newspaper, or in the food they have just fetched from the restaurant car. Travelling by train or by coach is in fact an extraordinary experience. Modern technology takes us along at a pace way in excess of anything experienced by our ancestors. Scene after scene unrolls itself outside the window, a panorama of infinite fascination. Yet how few people are fascinated by it!

Meditation helps us reclaim the freshness of life. Through meditation, we see once more with the wonder of a child, yet with the accumulated experience of a mature adult. We thus have the advantage of the two phases of our lives. Next time you travel, try to remain mindful of each new experience as it unfolds. Even when at the wheel of a car, many people say that when they reach journey's end the simple act of watching the road has been automatic; and they can remember little of what they have seen.

Be Mindful of States of Being

To be human is to experience moods. Sometimes we feel positive and optimistic about ourselves and about life, and at other times we feel the world is on top of us. Sometimes we feel like partying, at other times like staying quietly at home. Our physical energy levels fluctuate. At times we feel ready to go, at others ready to go only to the nearest chair. Our attitudes to things can change too. Our interests can fluctuate. And even more noticeable, our emotions and our feelings, the light and shade of daily life, can resemble a roller-coaster. Psychological research reveals that the way we are feeling can even influence our choice of colour. If we feel emotionally highly-charged – especially with anger – we may choose red. If we feel peaceful, we may go for blue.

Mindfulness allows us to become more aware of these changes and of the things that trigger them. Often, although we may protest that we don't know why we feel as we do, we have nevertheless missed an opportunity to find out. We have not been mindful of ourselves and of the situations in which we find ourselves. Why should this kind of mindfulness matter? The answers are apparent from what has been said so far. Self-awareness leads to self-understanding. Self-understanding enables us to manage our lives better, and to be more in control of ourselves and of how we react.

Just as mindfulness of the body enables us to become aware of muscular tensions the moment they occur, so mindfulness of our state of being allows us to become aware of psychological tensions the moment they occur. It is often at the moment of occurrence that we are best able to dispel the tension, and to recognize that by allowing ourselves to become tense in response, for example, to the challenges and difficulties during the working day, we render ourselves less able to cope with these challenges, and we do our psychological and physical health no good. In addition, if our state of mind prompts us to act inappropriately, frequently we find ourselves regretting it afterward, and having to apologize to colleagues or friends for our behaviour.

There is more to mindfulness of our state of being even than this. Mindfulness of being allows us an opportunity, in each moment, to recognize what it actually is to be alive. We may wish to parcel out our experience, regarding humdrum events in the working day of little consequence compared with hours spent doing the things we really want to do. Yet each moment, whether at work or at play, presents us with the opportunity of identifying how life expresses itself through us. I was once told by a meditation teacher that this recognition may be more readily grasped during difficult moments than during relaxed ones. Be this as it may, each experience that arises in life is an opportunity for this recognition, and an opportunity that is not to be missed.

MEDITATION 32: **Become Mindful in Sleeping and Waking**

As our practice of meditation continues to develop, mindfulness should extend not only throughout the waking day, but into sleep as well.

- *Try each night to watch the process of falling asleep. At first, this seems impossible. You may lose consciousness all too quickly, or else keep yourself awake in a determined attempt to watch what is happening. But with practice, part of the mind can remain restfully conscious to the threshold of sleep, and even perhaps beyond.*

- *The first thing you will notice if you do remain conscious is the hypnogogic state, an interlude where visions and highly creative thoughts pass rapidly through the mind (surrealist painters such as Salvador Dali claim that much of their inspiration comes from these bizarre hypnogogic thoughts and visions). We may lose consciousness after the hypnogogic state, but may nevertheless regain it with the onset of dreaming.*

- *Without sustained practice, consciousness is unlikely to extend throughout dreamless sleep, but you may become conscious just before waking, while in the so-called hypnopompic states, where similar visions and thoughts arise to those experienced while falling asleep.*

Mindfulness of Nature

Most devoted meditators develop a particular fondness for nature. This is perhaps because, by becoming closer to ourselves, we become closer to that unity of which we are all a part. Nature not only sustains us, but lives and breathes in us. The air in our lungs is the same as the air outside. The iron, copper and other chemicals in our body are identical to the same chemicals outside. The water in our bodies is the same water that flows through the rivers and the streams. The food in our bellies comes from the earth and returns to the earth. Our minds are full of the pictures painted by nature, the trees and the far hills, the scent of flowers and the song of the birds.

By following the meditative path, this awareness of nature develops by itself, and leads to a life-enhancing sensitivity to all sentient and even insentient beings, so that we are acutely aware that crushing an insect on the window instead of opening the window and letting it go free diminishes all life, and risks brutalizing ourselves. This sensitivity is increased by the meditations on the suffering of animals and plants (see Meditations 28 and 29; pp.87 and 89). But we can assist it further by meditating in the open where possible. When this is not feasible, many meditators like to bring leaves, twigs, shells and feathers into the house – honouring and respecting them as expressions of life. In one of the retreat centres I used to frequent, hidden in the wilds of the countryside, the master used to bring in the skulls and bones of dead sheep that he found on the hills. This initially surprised me, until I recognized that these relics of the life that had walked on those hills had a magical beauty of their own, and reminded us all that life ends in death, and that it is up to us to know the meaning of both of these states of being.

In the 19th century, the Romantic poets, Shelley, Keats, and Byron in particular, felt a wild affinity with the drama of wind and rain and thunderstorm. Nature poets such as Wordsworth, Tennyson, Emerson, and Walt Whitman all had an intensely mystical sense of their kinship with the Earth, recognizing that the life that animated them was the same life that animated all creation. So be mindful of nature. Watch the seasons. If you live in the city, surrounded only by man-made things, go into the countryside as often as you can, and when this proves impossible bring nature into the house, find something that has lived and bring it home with you. Try not to judge days as good or bad by the view of the weather that reveals itself as you draw back the curtains in the morning. All days are good days, all weathers have their purpose, all sunrises and sunsets have their charm.

Meditation 33 gives you another way in which you can be conscious of nature, and of the unity between your own body and the elements outside your window.

MEDITATION 33: **Be Mindful of the Elements**

For the ancients, there were only four elements. These were the four ways in which we experience the natural world. All things are solid (earth), liquid (water), hot or cold (fire or its absence) and gaseous (air). Centuries later, this is still how we experience the world – and indeed how we experience our own bodies. Because in addition to experiencing the elements outside us, we can also experience them inside us, as this meditation shows.

1   *Sit in meditation and become aware of your body as solid, sitting with weight upon your cushion. Stay with this awareness until it enters deep into your consciousness.*

2   *Next, become aware of your body as liquid, the seven-eighths of it that are water, and the blood flowing in your veins and arteries.*

3   *Become conscious of your body as heat, as the fire that goes with life. Become fully aware of the warmth that sustains you.*

4   *Become aware of yourself as air, as the air in your lungs and the oxygen in your blood. Become conscious of the air without which physical life would quickly become impossible.*

5   *Extend feelings of gratitude to the elements – outside and inside your body – that give you physical form and sustain that form.*

Direct Contemplation

Direct contemplation allows us to draw even closer to the realization of our unity with all of creation. Practised particularly in the Soto school of Zen Buddhism, it involves selecting, preferably outdoors, a particular object for meditative attention, and takes us further than the object meditations that we have looked at so far. The object chosen should be natural not man-made, and small enough to be observed without eye-movement, such as a stone.

All concepts about the object are discarded. It exists in its own right, independently of the labels we attach to it and of the thoughts we have about it. Even the words we use for its colour and shape and constituent elements are unknown to the object. It has the same right to existence that we have. It occupies its own space by right, just as we occupy our own space. It is warmed by the same sun as we are, and cooled by the same winds and the same rain. It owes us nothing, and asks nothing of us.

By freeing the mind from concepts, direct contemplation enables us to realize a state of equality with the object. We and it are fellow beings. And as contemplation deepens, the awareness dawns that the object exists not just out there but within our own consciousness. It is one with us, just as we are one with it. The boundaries are down. In both it and ourselves, the same natural forces are simply expressing themselves.

MEDITATION 34: **Practise Direct Contemplation**

There is a tendency when practising direct contemplation to select an object that we find attractive, a wild flower exquisite in its beauty or the fragile skeleton of a leaf, left over from Autumn. But attractive objects (and those we find repugnant) have far more concepts attached to them than neutral objects. Go instead for something that allows what is called content-less awareness. The object is simply there, and therefore worth our attention.

1 *Focus initially on your breathing, and when you feel centred, transfer your awareness to the object. Look at it, blinking as little as possible. Expect nothing and ask for nothing. You are simply expressing your perceptual relationship to the object.*

2 *Disregard any tricks that this perception may play. For example, you may fancy you see an aura around the object, but don't let this distract you.*

3 *Be aware that the object exists both of itself and in your own mind. Allow this sense of unity to develop.*

4 *After practising direct contemplation the world may seem strange, as if you are seeing it for the first time. This is fine, but it is difficult to function always in this acute awareness. Sit quietly and allow habitual perception to return.*

Building a Meditation Program

We've covered a number of different meditation techniques, and it's now time to look at how you can build all these into your meditation program.

Firstly, we must stress again the need for this program to be regular and consistent. Ideally, this means one (or perhaps two) sessions of meditation per day, at the same time and in the same place. Naturally, this isn't always possible. You may be away on holiday or on business, you may have family and friends visiting. There may be other demands that interfere with your program. Inevitably then, you may have to miss some days of regular practice. When this happens, try and turn your thoughts to meditation, even if you can't sit on your cushion, at other times during the day. Even five or ten minutes will help you to keep up the habit of daily practice. One day of missed practice quickly becomes two, and two becomes three, and then you are faced with the problem of picking up where you left off, which is never easy. So help yourself by finding just a few minutes, even when circumstances are most difficult, to close your eyes and turn your attention to your breathing.

If all else fails, meditate when you get to bed or when you awake in the morning. Purists may say that you should always sit in the proper position for meditation, and certainly it isn't good to make a habit of only meditating when you're lying down. But it is said, quite rightly, that we should be able to meditate in any position, sitting, standing or lying. This ensures that you can meditate whatever the situation.

But let's say you can have your meditation session most days. How should you use it? It's essential to have your root practice, and the most reliable one is meditation on the breathing, in the way we've described. Even if you are trying another practice, it's good to focus initially upon the breathing until the mind settles down and is ready to go on to something else. When you try some of the other practices we look at in the book, resolve to do so for a set period of time. For example, you may choose to work with one of them for seven or ten days, or longer. Give yourself a realistic chance to try them out. Then go back to working with the breath for a similar period of time, so that you can fully absorb the experience of the new method. Then switch back to it if you wish, though always keeping the breath as your root practice.

Mindfulness should be practised as often as possible each day. After a time, it becomes something of a habit, so little effort is involved. The results it brings in improved memory, in improved efficiency, and in greater enjoyment of life are sufficient in themselves to make you want to continue with it. Try as well to have short periods when you focus particularly on mindfulness, maintaining the silent commentary (see Meditation 8; p.41) on everything that you are doing. And try to be particularly mindful when walking, mindful of the movements of the body and of everything that presents itself to the senses as you walk.

There are usually opportunities even in daily life to focus on objects, both moving and static, and to try short periods of direct contemplation. Certainly you can sometimes use these practices as part of your daily meditation session, but make use of the brief opportunities for focusing and direct contemplation that regularly present themselves, and that we often waste in daydreaming or chattering or in flicking through television channels. Contemplation of spiritual symbols or of visualizations usually requires more time, and is best incorporated into your sitting meditation sessions as you wish.

If all this sounds as if meditation will take over your life, or intrude too much into other pursuits, nothing could be further from the truth. The mind is always active during waking hours. Simply ensure that it does things of value to you rather than wasting your time. Some meditation practices such as mindfulness are of such obvious practical value that few people should prove unwilling or unable to spend a few minutes a day deliberately practising them and enjoying the many benefits they bring.

MEDITATION 35: **Analyze your Program**

Try to identify any difficulties associated with your program. The most obvious one is probably that, as you are not a monk or in permanent retreat, it is all too easy for meditation to become a casualty of modern living, squeezed out between family, work, leisure and social engagements. When we are tired at night or in the morning, meditation tends to be put to one side. As we have seen, once the habit of meditation is broken, it becomes difficult to re-establish. Sometimes, having gained the benefits we seek from meditation, the motivation to carry on decreases, much as we might stop taking the tablets once we start to recover from a physical illness. So analyze your program from time to time in order to monitor what is happening.

- *Identify where you may not be fulfilling your program, then ask yourself why this should be. Were you too ambitious to begin with, and in consequence set yourself unrealistic targets? Have you become complacent after deriving early benefits from the practice? Does meditation have too low a priority in your life? Is there opposition from family or friends? Are there too many distractions in your life? Are you simply bored with meditation? Have you become disillusioned at your seeming lack of progress? Which areas of the program give you most difficulty? Can you identify why?*

Dealing with Boredom

Years ago, one of my meditation teachers told me that unless his pupils felt bored sometimes in meditation, they were not practising properly. He meant that most of us can sit happily for half an hour lost in thought. We can relax with our fantasies, our pleasant memories, and our ego-polishing. Meditation, by contrast, can be hard work. Focusing on the breathing and on keeping the mind clear can certainly become boring once the novelty wears off, and before we reach the state of tranquility.

So boredom is an important stage in the practice, and something to be worked through. As with your work on your other feelings, look at boredom. What is it? Where is it in the body? Why is it troublesome? Recognize that boredom is an attempt by the busy, chattering mind to regain control. And once you have worked through it, the mind is greatly strengthened as a result.

Monitoring the Days and Weeks

Looking back over the day and over the week is a powerful aid to the development of mindfulness and memory. Ideally meditators should keep a daily diary, recording each evening what has happened during the day, including a weekly review each weekend.

The spiritual and Western mystery traditions all emphasize the vital importance of these reviews, stressing that looking closely at what happens in life each day and each week helps you to become aware of both the richness and the subtlety of experience, and to wake from the half-sleep in which we go through so much of life. The spiritual traditions also view the daily and weekly reviews as a way of identifying when we may have missed opportunities to be of value in the world. Recognizing these missed opportunities should be used as an aid to learning about ourselves rather than a source of guilt or of feelings of inadequacy. After all, we cannot do everything. There are only 24 hours in a day and seven days in a week, and juggling the conflicting demands on our time is never easy. But the reviews help us make choices between these demands, and to recognize where our own strengths and weaknesses lie. The mystery traditions advise that the review of the day should sometimes be done backward, from evening to morning, and you can try this if you wish. It certainly leads to changed concepts about time.

MEDITATION 36: **The Review of the Day**

If you are an evening meditator, the review is best done after your session. Doing it just before the session can make your mind too busy for meditation.

- *Start by asking yourself if you remembered your dreams that morning and kept your dream diary. Go on from there. Recall events, and your reactions to them and your feelings about them. Recall also the motivation behind your actions and the consequences of them. Knowing that, come the evening, you are going to complete a review of the day helps you focus more on what happens during it.*

MEDITATION 37: **The Review of the Week**

If you keep a diary of your daily reviews, read through it on the weekend. If you don't, just think back across the week. Be objective with yourself during the review.

- *How have you used your time this week? Note successes and shortcomings. Note changes in mood. Look back to the beginning of the week and see what progress you have made in self-development. To what extent have you enhanced life during the week, not just for other people but for plants and animals and the environment?*

More on Dreams

At this point it's of value to see the difference that meditation and mindfulness, together with your dream diary, have made to your dream life. You may well notice that your dreams have become richer and easier to recall.

You may also have found that you now have lucid dreams, which stay in the mind long afterward. Carl Jung also speaks of "great" or "grand" dreams, which have a profoundly spiritual quality and appear to arise from the collective unconscious rather than from your personal unconscious. These dreams typically contain archetypal images such as the divine child, the wise old man, the earth mother, the hero, or the magician. (Most of these archetypes appear in the major arcana of the Tarot cards). Grand dreams also remain in the mind, and can be regarded as signposts on the path of spiritual development.

You may even have found that you have had so-called Out of Body Experiences (OBEs) during sleep, perhaps as an extension of a lucid dream. These experiences, for which there is no materialistic explanation, involve the apparent location of the consciousness outside the body. Those who have them sometimes report seeing their sleeping bodies on the bed, and even obtaining information about the outside world during the OBE which they could not have come by naturally.

MEDITATION 38: **Stay Mindful of Dreams**

Although bad dreams may be helpful in drawing our attention, symbolically, to things in our life of which we should be more aware or that we may need to change – for example needless fears and anxieties carried with us since childhood, repressed emotions or emotions that have become out of control – we rightly have no wish to go on remembering these dreams. We should learn from them – with the help of a psychotherapist if necessary – and once we have done so we should let them fade from memory. However, there are more positive and beautiful dreams that can teach us enduring lessons. How do we remain mindful of them? Sometimes they remain naturally in our memory thanks to the profound influence they have upon us, but at other times we either forget the details, or realize we are remembering memories *about* the dreams, rather than the dreams themselves.

- *Stay mindful of these dreams by re-entering them regularly. Notice again the colours, the scenery. If a house is involved, go inside, enter the rooms, look through the windows. If people are involved, remember how they looked and what they said to you. Recall the emotions that you felt at the time. Do not deliberately try to add to the dream, but if you spontaneously experience things that seem to belong to it, allow them to become part of the dream memory.*

chapter 3

Tranquility

Meditation involves three stages. The first of these stages, concentration, represents the essential groundwork for both sitting meditation and mindfulness. Once the meditator starts to develop light, objective, watchful concentration, the second stage of meditation, tranquility, arises of itself. Tranquility is the natural state of the mind. As soon as we no longer attend to the mental chatter that usually fills our heads, the mind settles into a deep sense of peace. This is sometimes referred to as "calm abiding", and is crucial in enabling the third stage of meditation, insight, to emerge, which is the subject of Chapter 4.

In calm abiding, we are simply in our own place, serene and untroubled, yet without a sense that this is anything we have done for ourselves. We have rediscovered what we have always been and always will be. Life is being lived and expressed through ourselves. None of these realizations is actually present during tranquility. If they were, we would once more be lost in thought, and the experience of tranquility would have disappeared. The realizations come later, when the meditation has finished and we are thinking back over it.

Experience Tranquility

Tranquility is simply there to be experienced. Nothing is done to obtain it beyond sitting in meditation and stilling the mind, and nothing is done with it when it arrives. It is not greeted with excitement or pride or self-justification. Any or all of these things immediately dissipate the experience. It is just a state of presence, no more and no less.

Yet tranquility does of course indicate progress in meditation. It is also during the tranquility experience that many of the benefits of meditation, both psychological and physical, begin to emerge. The meditator experiences a dimension of the mind that, although always present, has perhaps never previously become fully conscious. This dimension is experienced differently by different people, and it's important not to give preconceptions about it that may get in the way of the experience itself. Some people report seeing beautiful visions, others describe feeling in the presence of a loving spiritual power. At some point I myself re-live dreams that I seem to have had many years before, but never previously recalled (yet I know they are dreams, just as we know each morning we have been dreaming). But these are experiences that arise during tranquility, and must not be mistaken for tranquility itself, and they must not be grasped and held onto. If they are, tranquility is again lost, and we are simply daydreaming.

MEDITATION 39: **Avoid Trance**

This daydreaming can represent another potential obstacle to tranquility. The meditator may lose focused concentration, and instead settle into a trance-like state. Visions, and also psychic and mediumistic experiences may arise while in trance. All the great traditions emphasize that psychic abilities can develop as a result of spiritual development, but it is stressed that these abilities should not be seen as the purpose of meditation, but instead as potential distractions. Whether you have experienced tranquility or not, it is all too easy to fall into a trance state while meditating. This is a kind of dreamy, half-asleep condition, pleasant enough in itself, but definitely not the stuff of meditation.

1 *Be careful to recognize this trance state if it arises during your meditation. Dispel it by bringing your concentration very firmly back to your breathing or to your other point of focus.*

2 *At the end of a meditation session, think back over it. Did you slip into a trance on any occasion? Even if not in trance, did you become lost in any beautiful visions that arose?*

Visions are signs of progress in meditation. But once we allow ourselves to become absorbed in them, or to take them too seriously, we progress no further in meditation than seeing visions.

Maintain Tranquility

I am frequently asked how tranquility differs from the hypnotic trance. Having experienced both states, they could hardly be more different. Meditation is a state of alertness, the hypnotic trance is comparable to a drugged state, in which one is only dimly aware, and without any real sense of personal control. But once in tranquility, how does one maintain the state?

One does not try to maintain tranquility. The state is either there or it is not. A useful image is that of a mirror. Imagine that the mirror is covered with dust, so that no reflection can be seen in it. Now imagine that the dust is carefully cleared away, so that the mirror is bright and clear. Now it can reflect. The mirror produces the reflection of itself. All that the person responsible for cleaning it does is to restore the conditions in which it can reflect.

Similarly, all the meditator does is to remain focused. If tranquility arises, that is good. If it fades, that is not seen as bad. Seeing it as bad creates a feeling of loss, and that feeling becomes a major obstruction to the return of tranquility. The meditator does not pass judgement on whether tranquility is there or not, because to pass judgement is to slip back into thinking. All that happens is that the meditator stays focused and sits patiently on the cushion, not expecting, not even hoping, but just observing.

This may sound very passive, but the meditative mind is in

truth neither passive nor active. To be one or the other is to be pulled into oppositional thinking – either "I must refrain from doing anything" or "I must be doing something". Somewhere in between passive and active, there is a state just of being, and this is the state of tranquility.

Recognizing Tranquility

During tranquility, the mind abides in its timeless clarity, beyond conceptualizations and categorizations. But tranquility can involve several different levels. At the initial level, tranquility can be recognized as the dropping of everything that disturbs the mind. At a deeper level, it is dropping everything that distracts the mind. At a deeper level still, it can mean dropping attention even to the point of focus. The attention is still there, calm and bright, but the mind has entered a state of attention-less awareness. At the deepest level one is only aware of labels like "tranquility" when the meditation is over.

But don't try to define which level you're in during the session! If you do, tranquility is replaced by thinking.

Visualization

We are now ready to look at meditations involving visualizations. Even some experienced meditators say they have difficulty in visualizing. Others may even claim that they are quite unable to do so. The answer to these people is to remind them that they dream every night, and visualize clearly enough while doing so. Everyone can visualize. Like forgetting dreams, failure to visualize is largely a matter of losing a natural ability through misuse.

We may often have the impression that artists, who can draw and paint things skilfully from memory, are much better natural visualizers than the rest of us. But talk to any artist, and the chances are he or she will tell you they have had to work at developing their innate visualization skills. They will also tell you that the ability to pay attention to the world (we would call it mindfulness) is essential if one is to visualize. To remember how things look, one must first take the trouble to see them. Artists insist that the act of taking more interest in visual experience, in shapes and colours, in light and shade, is part of the act of seeing, as is the constant practice of trying to draw things from memory.

The meditations involving concentration on still and moving objects in Chapter 2 will have helped you with this process of seeing, and your work on mindfulness will have helped you further. Meditation 40 should also be of value.

MEDITATION 40: **Practise Visualization**

If you have difficulties with visualization, the best starting point is with geometrical forms. Geometrical forms are abstractions created by the human mind. They appear to originate at archetypal levels of inner awareness rather than from outward experience (we never see perfect circles, squares or triangles in nature). As such we can assume that they exist as latent constructs within our unconscious. Thus in visualizing them we are recognizing something that is already present in our own minds.

1 *Draw a circle (often regarded as a symbol of completion, in that it has no beginning and no end) in the colour green on a large sheet of white paper and place it at eye-level when you sit on your cushion.*

2 *Focus upon the circle until you feel you have it fixed in your mind. Close your eyes and try to hold the image in the inner space just above the eyes. When it fades or slips away to right or left, open your eyes and look again at the circle. Keep repeating the process.*

3 *When you have practised this (it may take several sessions) and can hold the image reasonably steadily in your mind's eye, change your visualization of the circle from green to red and then back again.*

4 *Experiment with other colours and geometrical shapes. As your ability to visualize develops, try visualizing objects, scenery or faces.*

Using a Mandala

Mandalas and yantras often feature in meditation. Much used in Buddhism, Jainism and Hinduism, a mandala is an arrangement of geometrical shapes in which figures of Buddhas, bodhisattvas or deities appear. In the absence of these figures the term yantra is usually used. One of the best known yantras is the *Sri Yantra*, a series of triangles within a circle said to symbolize the moment of creation of the visible world.

The meditator may focus on the mandala or yantra with open eyes, or visualize it in the forefront of the mind. The geometrical arrangements of a mandala or yantra are said to have an archetypal quality that allows them to act as a key to the unconscious and our enlightened being – the inner essence that the spiritual traditions tell us is our true nature. The mandala or yantra acts as the point of concentration and, with practise, is eventually held as a visualization.

Psychologists have noted the tendency of small children to draw circles and crosses, which indicates that these mandala-like shapes are natural to us. The famous psychotherapist Carl Jung found that during the process of healing, many of his patients drew their own mandalas. When he constructed his house in Switzerland, he did so in the form of a mandala. Living within the mandala was to Jung part of his journey of self-discovery.

MEDITATION 41: **Practise With a Mandala**

You can use the *Sri Yantra* or any other yantra or mandala that appeals to you. Or you can construct your own. If you wish to create your own mandala or yantra, don't expect to produce something that resonates with you first time. Prepare a number of sheets of paper with large (if possible perfect) circles on them, and allow the mind to create what it will out of one of them after each meditation. Wait until you feel one of them represents aspects of your inner world before you use it. Alternatively, you can construct your mandala outdoors, using natural objects like rocks and stones, and sit within it while meditating. The effect of the yantra or mandala may be entirely at the unconscious level. You may only become aware of this effect over the course of time.

• *When you have the mandala or yantra of your choice, put it where you can see it at eye-level while sitting on your cushion. Look at it steadily and without preconceptions. Don't try to bring meaning to it or to see meaning in it. Allow meaning, if it will, to arise from it (a yantra, which does not contain figures, is often more appropriate to begin with than a mandala). Just use the image in front of you as the focus for your meditation.*

Using Sound in Meditation

There are certain sounds, such as shamanic drumming, that have a measurable effect upon brain function, and that can be used to induce altered states of consciousness. These have their value, but if sounds are used in meditation, their purpose is rather different. Two examples are the bell and the singing bowls, used extensively in the Eastern traditions. The bell is self-explanatory. The singing bowls also produce a bell-like note when struck, but usually the wooden striker is drawn smoothly and continually around the rim of the bowl, rather as we move a wet finger around the rim of a wine glass, until it produces an ethereal singing sound. If we listen attentively to the sound, we recognize that it contains simultaneously both an upper and a lower note.

When used in meditation, the bell or the bowl are sounded briefly at the start of the session. The meditator then listens to the sound as it gradually fades into the distance. In Hindu thinking the sound, like a candle flame when it is blown out, does not die, but moves into another dimension. As it does so, it takes with it the mind of the meditator. In the case of the singing bowl, the lower note represents the physical world and the upper note the spiritual world. The former dies away before the latter.

Sound can also be used in the form of a mantra. In Hinduism, each god has his or her own mantra, the repetition of which is said

MEDITATION 42: **Use Sound**

A bell or a singing bowl used at the start of meditation helps to settle the mind. If you choose to use one of these, try to obtain one specially made for the purpose, which produces the most effective note. You may also like to chant a mantra. In formal meditation sessions the focus is on the mantra instead of the breath. A mantra can also be carried in the mind during the day, and repeated silently whenever the mind wishes to become clear or peaceful. In the Orthodox Church, it is said that the Jesus Prayer should be taken into the heart, where it goes on repeating itself even below the threshold of awareness.

1 *To note the physical effect of sound, use the Sanskrit sound "Om", said to be the primal sound. This is pronounced A-U-M (phonetically R-OO-MM). Take a deep breath and sound the "A" deep down in the solar plexus, the "U" in the chest, and the "M" high up in the head. This is done by making the first sound as if in the back of the throat, the second sound as if up near the palette, and the third sound vibrating at the lips.*

2 *Complete a dozen repetitions of this sound. Notice the effect upon the body and the mind. The body often seems to be tingling with a kind of inner vibration, while the mind is clear and energized.*

to attract his or her divine energy. Such mantras are in Sanskrit, said to be a sacred language and to contain the primal sounds that when uttered by Brahma brought the world of form into being, and the meditator is told to concentrate upon the sound itself, not upon any meaning that the words may have. Tibetan Buddhist mantras are in Tibetan, while Arabic, also said to be a sacred language, is used when calling upon the name of Allah. In Christianity, Roman Catholics use the Hail Mary, while Russian and Greek Orthodox churches use the Jesus Prayer ("Lord Jesus Christ have mercy upon me a sinner").

Mantras can be chanted or repeated loudly or silently to oneself. As with any other point of focus, they give the mind a centre of concentration. It is said that if you are given a mantra within one of the great spiritual traditions, you must receive it in the course of a ceremony that empowers the mantra for you, and gives you clear guidance upon exactly how it should be pronounced and used. But it is also sometimes said that you can invent your own mantra (for example a word like "peace"), and use it very effectively. Certainly, both received and invented mantras can act equally well as centres of concentration, though the sounds of the former may indeed have a special effect upon the mind. Much may depend upon whether or not you have a teacher who can give you your mantra (said to be chosen to fit your personality).

Compassion and Healing

The link between mind and body is clearly established by modern science. In addition to the role of the mind in activating the body, it is also responsible for bodily tensions, strains and misuse. Latest estimates from some members of the medical profession suggest that as much as one third of physical illnesses may be psychological in origin. To this we could add the effects that the mind has upon itself in terms of anxiety, depression, and stress. Meditation is not a cure for the damage we do to ourselves (and to others), but it does help the healing process, and does so in ways unique to itself. I have often felt in my work in psychology, in spite of all the strengths of this great pathway into the human mind provided by this subject, that meditation is the best practice I have to teach, and the best route toward self-understanding.

How does meditation assist healing? The answer is that it does so at unconscious levels. The very practice of meditation is healing, without our trying to do anything special with the practice. The development of compassion toward others and toward ourselves that arises from meditation is also a major aid to healing. Compassion leads to peacefulness and gentleness, to greater patience and tolerance toward others and ourselves, to greater understanding, to greater insight into the problems and sufferings and challenges that we all face.

In addition we can build specific healing sessions into our meditation program. Some experts who work with visualization exercises in healing advocate picturing the body's defences (personalized into whatever form one chooses) repelling and destroying whatever it is that plagues the body. Another very important aid is to visualize oneself becoming well again. Too often when we are sick we get into the habit of thinking of ourselves as sick. For example, people with bad backs typically see themselves as handicapped by back pain, and as moving stiffly and with great difficulty. People with a debilitating illness think of themselves as debilitated. People with depression think of themselves as depressed. Through meditation, these negative thoughts can be replaced by positive ones. The woman with a bad back can visualize herself (either from within her body or as if she is observing herself from outside) running freely along a beach, or doing all the things she currently cannot do. A man with a debilitating illness can visualize himself strong and well again. People with depression can visualize themselves as happy once more, and enjoying the things that happy people enjoy.

Meditation can also help with pain management. The meditator learns to focus upon breathing rather than upon pain. The pain is still there, but no longer at the forefront of awareness. Some teachers advocate actually turning the attention to the pain, observing it dispassionately and allowing it to soften and relax.

MEDITATION 43: **Assist Healing in Others**

The spiritual traditions have long believed prayer can assist healing in others as well as in oneself. Spiritual healers also believe they can send distant healing to those in need. Science has hitherto largely rejected these claims, but recent research in American hospitals has demonstrated that groups of cardiac and AIDS patients prayed for or sent distant healing by prayer and healing groups show significantly better progress than control groups who are not.

- *To try to send healing during meditation, focus clearly and steadily upon the image of the patient. With each out-breath, visualize yourself sending streams of healing white light to this image. Practise this over several sessions.*

- *You can also visualize your image of the patient receiving the energy, and beginning to look better as a result.*

- *If the patient believes distant healing is effective, his or her own mind may also assist the healing process. If you wish to explore your own part in the healing, the patient should not know the time at which your meditation takes place. Check later if he or she feels any particular effect at this time.*

More on Meditation and Healing

Meditation can be used in conjunction with positive affirmations to assist psychological or physical healing. The affirmation can be used as a mantra, and repeated silently to oneself or out loud as the point of focus throughout a meditation session.

Positive affirmations consist of positive statements about oneself. For example, in dealing with depression, one might use "My spirits are rising". When assisting the healing of a damaged knee one might repeat "My knee is moving freely again". When dealing with shyness, one might repeat "I am open and confident with people". Choose whatever form of words seems right for you and for the problem with which you are dealing. But keep the affirmation very simple. The unconscious is far more likely to get the message, and pass healing energy on to the wanted place within the body should the problem be a physical one, if you don't overburden it with affirmations containing more than one instruction. If you want to use several affirmations, use them separately. You can use the affirmation as often as possible during the day, like a mantra, but unlike mantras where the sound is important, try to pay full attention to the actual meaning of the words.

To achieve the best effect, you can follow the affirmation with a visualization of it taking effect – for example of yourself acting confidently when speaking to a room full of people. You can use

MEDITATION 44: **Practise Self-Healing**

Positive affirmations work best if you believe in them, so choose affirmations you find credible rather than ones requiring instant miracles. When dealing with a complex problem, work on it step by step, affirmation by affirmation. Don't make a huge effort to believe in your affirmation. Strenuous mental effort is incompatible with meditation. Hold the affirmation lightly and clearly in the mind. Feel confident of its value. And don't expect immediate results. I must stress again that meditation is not a cure-all. It is a way of putting yourself in a good position for cure to take place.

1 *Practise the "favourite place" visualization (see p.132) by calling to mind the general scene, then look closely at each detail, clarifying it in turn. Hold the visualization and allow the feelings associated with that place to arise. When they do so, imagine either walking into the scene, or see yourself doing so objectively.*

2 *If you find difficulty "walking into" the scene, the Tarot cards can help. Choose a card that illustrates a place where you would like to be, and an archetype who you feel can be of psychological or spiritual help. Place it at eye-level and focus on it in meditation.*

3 *When the image is clear, close your eyes and hold it as a visualization. Visualize or feel yourself walking into the picture.*

affirmations when trying to send healing to others too.

Another way of using healing meditation is to visualize your favourite place – perhaps in the mountains, by the seaside, in the woods, in a quiet room or in an art gallery. Wherever it happens to be, build up the visualization in as much detail as you can, and then visualize yourself relaxed and well within this chosen spot. Or you can visualize yourself, either in your favourite place or on your meditation cushion, bathed in healing light from some spiritual source. Many people prefer to visualize this light as white, but you can suit the colour to your needs of the moment. Thus blue is good for relaxation, green for feeling rejuvenated, red for energy, orange for spirituality. Sit as if at the base of a cone of this light streaming down from above, filling you and the immediate space in which you are sitting. Try to wear something in the chosen colour at the time and afterward.

Finally there is evidence that laughing and smiling release desirable chemicals into the blood stream. Many Buddhist teachers insist that the meditator should sit with a half-smile on the lips (not difficult once the meditation relaxes you, and very easy when you enter tranquility), and this smile should therefore have physical as well as psychological benefits. Try to smile more in daily life – at other people, at things you like, at your reflection in a mirror or a shop window. Smiles light up the rest of the world, and tell your unconscious that you intend to be happy.

MEDITATION 45: **Deal with Low Self-Esteem**

Many psychologists and psychotherapists agree that the inability to value oneself is the root of many psychological and perhaps physical problems. Low self-esteem or low self-acceptance have a destructive effect upon one's spirits, upon mental and physical energy, upon relationships with others, and upon one's general effectiveness in life. Each of the meditations we have mentioned in connection with healing can help raise self-esteem, or you can combine them as follows.

1 *Choose a positive affirmation that seems right for you. "Of course I can" is a good general one, but you may wish to be more specific, for example "I can succeed at .....", "I think well of myself", "People will value me". Use the affirmation as often as you can.*

2 *Picture yourself in a range of situations where low self-esteem has been a particular problem in the past, and see yourself as behaving effectively. Notice that people smile at you and nod approvingly.*

3 *See yourself bathed in a colour that you associate with success and popularity.*

4 *Visualize yourself back in childhood, and doing well in the situations where you felt a failure.*

Habits and Relationships

Meditation, done consistently and with commitment, can be a life-changing practice. It yields subtle changes in consciousness in addition to its many other benefits. In becoming more psychologically and emotionally balanced, and more peaceful and more tranquil, the meditator may find that habits he or she has been trying for years to discontinue now disappear of themselves. They lose their appeal, and the hold that they have upon mind and body. By reducing stress, meditation may also remove the actual need for habits, such as smoking and excessive drinking, that have hitherto been used to combat the tensions of daily life.

Meditation can also be specifically used to help overcome habits. There are two ways in which this can be done. Firstly, the meditator can try to identify within him or herself the causes of the habit concerned. (This is dealt with in Chapter 4, where we look at insight.) Secondly, the meditator can use positive affirmations and visualizations. There is an old saying that is respected within modern psychology: as we think, so we are. If we think of ourselves as succeeding, or as acquiring desirable qualities and abilities, we are part way to making these things into realities. The right approach is one of modesty and realism, wishing only to achieve something that assists our self-development.

MEDITATION 46: **Break Habits and Improve Relationships**

The first part of this meditation uses positive affirmation and visualization to overcome unwanted habits. The second part touches on another troublesome area – difficulties in relationships. These may arise either from the nature of the people with whom you have to deal, or from friction within otherwise loving and satisfactory relationships – between partners or within the family.

1 *For an unwanted habit, such as smoking, choose a positive affirmation, for example "I'm strong enough to stop". Note that you affirm the quality needed in order to stop, rather than merely affirming that you will stop. In addition, visualize yourself in situations where you usually take out a cigarette, and see yourself as not doing so or even wanting to do so. If a feeling of craving arises, stop the visualization, return to your breathing, and when the craving subsides, go back to the visualization.*

2 *The* metta *(loving kindness) meditation described in Chapter 1 (see Meditation 12; p.50) is helpful in dealing with difficult relationships, or problems within good relationships. Supplement this by visualizing problem situations, and see yourself handling them more sensitively. Arouse the feeling of understanding the other person and their difficulties, and of wanting them to be happy. If this seems hard, what is it in you that makes it hard?*

Insight

Insight, the third stage in the process of meditation, concerns the self-awareness that emerges when the meditator abides for any length of time in tranquility. It is impossible to describe this self-insight. It is essentially something to be experienced rather than written and read about. But certain generalities are possible, together with the associated meditative practices. In the following pages we shall attempt to outline both generalities and practices.

Once the tranquility stage of meditation becomes established, insights tend to emerge of themselves. These can either be disregarded along with distractions, or they can be observed and noted. Such insights may not always be the ones we expect, and it is possible to feel existential fear if, for example, they reveal that much of what we take to be ourselves is no more than a bundle of conditioned responses that must be laid aside if we wish to experience the pure mystery of being. Other insights may bring a sense of bliss similar to that met with in mystical experience. But whatever arises, the meditator observes it without judgement. What exists exists, and what has no real existence does not exist. All else can be a form of self-delusion.

What Has Been Learned So Far?

Meditation isn't like other forms of learning. Usually when we learn something we make steady progress. We may forget things and have to go back and revise them, but for the most part, progress is on a visible upward curve. However, with meditation progress is difficult to measure. Sometimes it seems as if we slip back. The circumstances and our state of mind when we meditate all play such an important part in the experience, that it is often difficult to recognize whether an apparent lack of progress is due to the intrusion of worldly affairs or to our role as a meditator.

We mentioned earlier that progress may sometimes be taking place when we are least aware of it. A few minutes of stillness during a very unsettled meditation may teach us more than half an hour of stillness at a time when life is proceeding smoothly. But nevertheless there will often be relatively long periods when we feel not only to be getting nowhere, but to be losing any gains that we may already have made. How do you keep going during these times? The first thing to recognize is that it is during difficult or over-excited episodes in life that we most need to meditate. If our minds were not difficult to control at such times, then we would have no need of meditation. It is precisely because our minds are so wayward, and so relatively unsuccessful at self-control, that we need to meditate.

The second thing is to look at the strength of your motivation. Has meditation simply become a habit, 20 minutes or half an hour to be got through each day in order to feel virtuous, regardless of whether concentration is there or not? If so, it is important to look again at motivation. Re-program yourself. Recapture the motivation with which you first began to practise. Go over again the reasons for meditating and the benefits it brings. Strengthen your resolve to stay focused and concentrated. And if you have become impatient with yourself, remember the old saying that time means nothing in this practice. We cannot set the idea of progress against the amount of time spent on that progress, as we do in other areas of learning.

So what should you have learned by now? Certainly the various techniques, even if you feel dissatisfied with the way in which you are practising them. You should have learnt the importance of concentration, and of the ability to maintain this concentration at least for a short time during some sessions. You should be familiar with the different ways in which you can use the breathing, and with the way in which visualization can be incorporated into meditation, whether for health or other reasons. You should be aware of the use of sound, of mantras, of mandalas and yantras. You should be clear on how to construct a meditation program and how to carry out reviews of the day and of the week. You should also be clear as to the importance of mindfulness, and the way in which dreams can be recalled and your dream life developed. You should have a feeling for how compassion can arise from meditation, and how the *metta* practice can help arouse this compassion and help to improve relationships. And you should be aware of the relationship between the conscious and unconscious levels of the mind and between the mind and the body.

If you have not been doing so, it is worthwhile going back at this point and looking again at the earlier chapters and meditations. Some of the latter should be part of your meditation program. Spend a little time recognizing any difficulties you may be having in your practice, and try to identify the reasons for them and the ways in which you can best work upon them.

When you are happy with your progress, and you feel ready to begin the third stage of meditation, try the following meditation. The practice uses thoughts as the focus of awareness. This is an advanced form of meditation, and presupposes that the meditator has progressed to the point where he or she can observe thoughts objectively, as if they are independent of the observer, and without becoming distracted by them.

MEDITATION 47: **You Are Not Your Thoughts**

In Meditation 4 (see p.25) the meditator watched the coming and going of thoughts, the following practice takes the watching of thoughts to the insight level of meditation.

1   *Sit in meditation, focusing upon the breath. Once in tranquility, turn your attention to your thoughts. Watch each thought as it arises, and the space between each one. These spaces may be long or short. Sometimes you may feel that a thought is trying to break into awareness, but lacks the strength to do so. Watch the thoughts that do emerge.*

2   *Are these thoughts random? Or is there some pattern to them? Notice chains of associations. What themes arise? Note these themes and consider them after the meditation, in the way detailed in the next section (see pp.142-3).*

3   *Finally, are you your thoughts? Are you still there in the spaces between thoughts?*

Examination of Your Thoughts

Meditation 47 asked you to watch your thoughts and notice the chains of associations and the themes that arise. This isn't easy. Thoughts can be very beguiling. Sometimes it seems as if the thought processes deliberately set out to capture the attention of the meditator. Happy memories, enticing fantasies, memories of urgent things one has forgotten to do, bright ideas, anxieties, hopes and expectations all surface, clamouring for attention.

But the experienced meditator refuses to be beguiled. Even thoughts that carry a strong emotional charge are simply, along with the emotion, observed from outside. In the course of this observation, many insights arise into the nature of one's thinking and into thinking in general. These insights are not pursued until after the meditation, when they can be examined dispassionately. They may reveal for example the trivial, random nature of much thinking. They may show the way in which one thought leads to another, which leads to another, setting up the long chains of associations that seem to go nowhere. They may show how many thoughts are linked to the ego – pride in things achieved, resentment at apparent slights received from others, self-justifications, plans to benefit oneself, worries about material possessions. They may show how many are connected to the past or the future, while the present becomes lost somewhere in between.

The superficial, self-related nature of much of this thinking may be surprising. Equally surprising may be the prevalence of thoughts about sex, and of worries over minor issues. These insights reveal not only the wasteful and unproductive nature of much of our thinking, but the predispositions and attitudes with which we face the world. Why is there perhaps so much thought about oneself and so little about others? So much about possessions, owned or coveted, and so little about spiritual matters? Why is there perhaps so little compassion, charity and love in one's thinking, so little real creativity, so little sensitivity?

However, there may also be much that is of value: promising lines of thought, care and concern for family and friends and for the under-privileged, insights into the reason for difficulties in meditation, and insights into how practice can be improved. Such things show a much more productive and enlightened level to our thinking.

Having looked at the details of your thinking, examine the process of thought itself. From where do thoughts arise? One moment the mind is clear, the next moment a thought is present. From where does it come? Can we ever know? If not, why not? Is it possible to trace thoughts back to their point of origin? Can the thoughts be said to come from ourselves or from outside ourselves? And what of those inspired thoughts that surprise us, and leave us puzzling at our ability to think so creatively?

MEDITATION 48: **You Are Not Your Body**

Meditations 48 and 49 were introduced in Chapter 1 (see Meditation 5; p.27). We can now take them further to help us with self-awareness. In part this meditation consists of repeating "I am not my thoughts, I am not my body". If we are our body (including the brain), when the body dies we die. Meditation helps us explore the notion of whether or not we are this body.

1   *Turn your attention from your breath to your body. Allow your awareness to travel over it. This body changes each day; after some eight years every cell has been renewed. Are you this ever-changing body?*

2   *The brain also changes and renews itself over this eight-year cycle. Can you possibly be this brain? If you are, why is it you remember your life more than eight years ago?*

3   *If you are not your body, who are you?*

Do not allow this meditation to disorientate yourself in any way. Of course you are your body and your brain and your thoughts. It is simply that you are not only these things. They are transitory aspects of yourself. Over-identification with them can impede your recognition of what lies behind them.

MEDITATION 49: **You Are Not Your Feelings**

If you are not your thoughts and not your body, are you your feelings? Feelings, often connected with emotions, are a major part of life. We feel good, we feel bad and so on. As with thoughts and the body, we can look at these feelings.

1 *Start your meditation as usual, then turn your attention to how you feel at this moment. Relaxed? Happy? Sad? Neutral? What is this feeling? Where is it? Notice how looking at it can change it in some way. In what way?*

2 *Be aware of how feelings come and go.*

3 *Are you these feelings?*

This meditation does not suggest that feelings are bad. Feelings are part of the rich colour of life, and life would be dull and flat without them. The problem arises when we allow negative feelings to control us, leading to unnecessary fear, anxiety, anger, resentment and frustration. Over-identification with our feelings can mean that we cling to negative states of mind long after we should have put them aside. Seeing negative feelings as transitory states helps to keep them in perspective.

Examination of Emotions and Feelings

Emotions and feelings (the two are intimately connected, although it is possible to have feelings about something without an attendant emotional charge) can arise as frequently as thoughts in meditation. Sometimes we feel emotional for no apparent reason as soon as we start to sit. Or an emotion may suddenly sweep over us during the sitting. Sometimes people sob or laugh uncontrollably during meditation. Often these emotions spark off thoughts. We may try to identify why we feel emotional. Or the emotion may trigger off related thoughts. Conversely, thoughts may trigger emotions. We remember an argument with an unreasonable (from our perspective) colleague and immediately anger arises, or a feeling of bewilderment at his or her behaviour. We may think of a loved one, and a sudden wave of tenderness and longing comes over us. Or we may think of a planned holiday and experience immediate excitement.

As with thoughts, the experienced meditator observes these emotions and feelings without becoming swamped by them. This doesn't imply an emotional coldness or an attempt to repress our affective life. The emotions and feelings are experienced by us (otherwise they would not exist), and no attempt is made to dampen them. But our attitude toward them when in meditation should be one of curiosity rather than involvement.

Emotions and feelings are of value and of interest, and thus in meditation are watched in a state of mind that allows them to be understood. Their texture becomes more apparent. No emotion is rejected. All are simply observed. No emotion or feeling is judged. That may come after the meditation, when certain emotions and feelings may be seen as unworthy and others as life-enhancing. For the present, they are just watched, with the same attention given to any other point of focus in meditation.

As meditation progresses, emotions and feelings, like thoughts, arise less often. Sometimes memories of difficult past experiences may come to mind, but instead of arousing embarrassment or anger, they arise and pass away in the limitless space of one's own mind. It is not that the memories no longer matter, just that they matter in a quite different way. Thoughts, emotions and feelings are no longer in control of the meditator, with his or her mind the seeming victim. They are seen as part of the wonderful tapestry of life, as part of what makes us human. But they are no longer seen as the tapestry itself, or as our humanity itself. They arise and pass away. What lies beyond and behind this play of inner experience?

The meditator can thus look for the origin of emotions and feelings. Like thoughts, they seem to arise from emptiness and return to emptiness. What is this emptiness? Can it be experienced? If so, what is our relationship to it?

The Use of Koans

Koans are the most intriguing and puzzling of all aids (some would say hindrances!) to the insight stage of meditation. Koans are essentially enigmatic statements or questions that make no logical sense. Used particularly in the Rinzai school of Zen Buddhism, they are given individually by the master to his or her pupils, who then use them as their focus in meditation. Koans have a graded level of difficulty and the master always selects the koan appropriate to the pupil's stage of development. Only when the koan is solved (resolved is a better word) to the satisfaction of the master is the pupil given a further koan on which to work.

Why are koans of use in meditation, and often used in Rinzai Zen in preference to other points of focus? One simple answer is that koans drive the mind beyond the limits of logical, linear thinking, thus leading to a breakthrough in which the mind experiences a sudden realization of what underlies the thought processes that habitually dominate it. But like all simplifications, this answer is only partly true. There is more to the koan than this, and the pupil is warned by the master not to embark upon koan meditation with preconceptions of what it is expected to do.

The best-known koan is "What is the sound of one hand clapping?". There is no logical answer. Even the answer "silence" would be wrong, because silence is not a consequence of clapping.

There are 48 koans in the *Mumonkan* (*The Gateless Gate*), and 100 in the *Hekiganroku* (*The Blue Cliff Record*), which are the two best-known collections of koans. All koans in the two major collections have brief stories associated with them, together with commentaries by later Zen masters, which are as enigmatic as koans themselves. Usually the master gives the pupil "Mu" as a first koan. The story surrounding "Mu" is that Joshu, the 9th-century Chinese master, was asked "Does a dog have Buddha nature?" To which he replied "*Mu*" ("*Wu*" in Chinese). On the face of it, "*Mu*", which can be translated as "no-thing", would seem to indicate that a dog does not have Buddha nature, but "*Mu*" is a negative beyond both positive and negative. So what did Joshu mean?

The pupil focuses on "Mu", until a sudden insight into its meaning appears to arise. At the next interview with the master, the pupil gives this answer. The master listens, probably gives a shake of the head, and rings the bell that signifies that the interview is over. The insight is incorrect, and the pupil returns to the meditation cushion to try again. This process may go on for weeks, months or even longer, until one day, perhaps wordlessly (it is said that the master can tell whether insight has been achieved as soon as the pupil enters the interview room), the pupil satisfies the master, and is then given another koan on which to work.

Understanding the Conundrum

What kind of answer might the pupil have given to the "Mu" koan? The only way to know is to work on the koan yourself. The value of the koan is the process that leads to the answer. The answer without this process is meaningless. We are not talking about the kind of question found in an examination paper, to which there is only one acceptable answer and which could be copied from the person sitting in front. The koan is a mind-exercise, and we can get no benefit from it without doing it ourselves.

One of the most helpful passages in the various commentaries to the koans is provided by the Zen master Mumon on the subject of Joshu's famous "oak tree" koan. Joshu was asked "What is the meaning of Bodhiddharma [the Indian Zen Patriarch] coming to China?", to which Joshu answered "The Oak tree in the garden". What would your answer be? To help you, Mumon (in Sekida's translation of the *Mumonkan*) wrote:

Words cannot express things
Speech does not convey the spirit.
Swayed by words one is lost;
Blocked by phrases, one is bewildered.

The question put to Joshu can be seen as "What is the purpose of Buddhism?" Or of any spiritual path? Difficult to answer in words!

MEDITATION 50: **Look Into a Koan**

Koan meditation requires the presence of a Zen master, who has personally resolved the koan, and who is thus able to assess the pupil's progress. However, provided the pupil does not become carried away with any insights that arise and assume the koan has been resolved, practise with koans is helpful for stilling the mind and observing whatever arises into the stillness.

1 *Let us assume that you work with Joshu's "Mu". A Ch'an (Chinese Zen) master instructed me to hold the koan in the mind, like something sweet. "Do not ask yourself for the answer" he insisted, "ask the koan". Another master told me to assume I was asking the koan to a wise friend "who sat opposite but never answered".*

2 *Whichever of these methods appeals to you, play with the koan rather than set off as you would if tackling a logical problem. It is said that as you play with the koan, turning it over in the mind, eventually it becomes "a great ball of doubt", and a sense of urgency to resolve it arises.*

3 *You can either think of "Mu" as "No-thing" or simply as "Mu". Does Joshu's answer mean that a dog has Buddha nature (potential enlightenment) and that Buddha nature is "no-thing"?*

MEDITATION 50: *continued*

4   *An advantage of the koan is that even outside sitting meditation it can become like a valued companion. "What is no-thing?" "Is a tree no-thing?" "Am I no-thing?" Do not expect any insights that arise to have obvious connections to the question itself.*

5   *You may also like to try the following koan, which is classified within Rinzai Zen meditation as a* Gonsen Koan, *and said to open up a hidden world of beauty and wisdom. The question "Speech and silence are concerned with subject and object. How can I transcend both subject and object?" is followed by the answer "I always think of Konan [a province in China] in March. Partridges chirp among the fragrant blossoms."*

Do you see it? Simply keep the question in mind, and observe the insight that arises from the answer.

In addition to paradoxical questions or statements, some koans involve a dialogue of questions and answers between the pupil and his or her teacher. One pupil asked his Zen master "What is the Great Way?" The master replied, "It is right before you." "Then why don't I see it?" enquired the pupil. "Because you are thinking of yourself." answered the master.

The Method of Inquiry

The conception of "great doubt" (or "great spirit of inquiry") is particularly stressed in traditions that follow the path of *gnana yoga* – the spiritual practice designed to encourage the development of knowledge. Knowledge in this context means not only book-learning but the intuitive wisdom that arises from deep inward exploration. One starts these practices with "great faith" – the inner conviction that an answer awaits the earnest spiritual seeker – and as the search continues the spirit of inquiry grows until it provides the energy that leads to the breakthrough into spiritual realization. Faith is then replaced by knowing. This is the pearl of great price of which Christ speaks, the Holy Grail of the Western mystery tradition, the Kingdom of Heaven, whether experienced in this world or in worlds to come.

The spirit of inquiry, once it develops, is always there, in waking and in sleeping, in meditation and in daily life. The koan, having presented itself stays with us. All koans are different, and unlock increasingly illuminating levels of the mind, but all koans have in common the fact that they are questions about the essential nature, meaning and purpose of life. In truth, life itself is the koan, this mysterious, self-contradictory experience that is given to us. From where and whence is it given, and why is it given? The meditator, asking his or her koan, wants to know.

Who Am I?

In effect, all koans are linked in some way to the fundamental existential question "Who Am I?". The question seems strange to most non-meditators, who are inclined to insist "Certainly we know who we are!". But do we? There is a practice, developed by Western Zen teachers, that places two pupils sitting opposite each other. The teacher rings a bell, and one pupil invites the other to "Tell me who you are." For five minutes the latter tries to answer. Then the bell rings, and the second pupil puts the request to the first pupil: "Tell me who you are." After five minutes, the bell rings again, and the questioning reverts to the first pupil. For the duration of the session, the question goes back and forth in this way. The questioner never responds to any of the answers that are given. There is only the question.

Typically, a pupil initially responds to the request with factual information, such as names, professional details, marital status, parenthood, age, sex, hobbies etc. But the questioner keeps insisting: "Tell me who you are." After a time the responses move away from personal details to personal characteristics: "I'm the kind of person who ....", "I get upset about ...", "I guess I'm a pretty extroverted sort of character" and so on.

But after the exercise has been under way for some time, the answers begin to peter out and may finally cease altogether. The

What Are Insights?

What do we mean by insights, and how are they recognized? Insights provide sudden leaps of understanding that lead to clarity. And through them we see what previously was obscure. An insight may appear novel, or may be something we seem always to have known but to have long forgotten.

Don't look too critically at insights. Often people dismiss as absurd in the light of science insights into areas of being that are in reality outside the scope of modern science. Allow insights to stand by themselves. They may arise from intuition (inner teaching), and only intuition can know their truth or otherwise.

Don't become over-excited if insights appear true. Savour and absorb them. But except in the case of great illuminations, allow time to assess their value.

pupil is faced with the realization that he or she does not know the answer. Sometimes this realization is very emotional: "I don't know, I don't know!" shouts the pupil. But if the "don't know" comes from the heart, this is an important breakthrough. Having exhausted all the labels that become attached to the self over the years, the pupil realizes that none of them represents who he or she really is. Sometimes this insight causes anger, sometimes tears. Either way, it reveals that the question has stripped away the false veneer that hides us from our real selves.

At a deep level, of course you know who you are. But who you are is an experience, not a formula. It must be experienced, really and deeply (the teacher, in the interview that follows, can always see through pretences), if the request is to be answered, and the koan "Who am I?" resolved (at least for the moment!).

Letting Go

Don't make a big effort to put insights into words. Words can sometimes be a hindrance on the meditative path. If we wish to define and analyze insights, we are thrown back upon words, and as the Zen master Mumon has reminded us, "Words cannot express them". Insights often illuminate at a level beyond words, and it is this illumination that stays with us.

Avoiding the temptation to try to express insights in logical terms is an example of letting go of unhelpful thoughts. At any stage of meditation, remind yourself to "let it go" – even repeating the phrase softly to yourself – when thoughts or emotions become too intrusive.

However experienced we are, all meditators other than masters (perhaps even masters) find that mental chatter periodically tries to reassert itself, especially if we become rather complacent and cease to be watchful. Let it go.

MEDITATION 51: **Make an Existential Discovery**

The "Who am I?" question does not necessitate two people. You can work on it yourself, using the question as your koan. Since this is perhaps the ultimate koan, we can none of us expect to come up with answers that would satisfy the Zen master. But he or she would not wish to prevent us from trying – provided we do not cling to any of our answers as if they are final. If they ring true for us, they are signposts on the path, but no more than signposts.

1   *As with all koans, approach "Who am I?" with an intrigued curiosity (as if you have been given a very interesting puzzle to solve). Treat it lightly. It is not a matter of life and death – at least in any sense in which we normally understand life and death. It is not something to fear. Whatever answers arise, they cannot alter who you are, they can only alter misconceptions about who you are. Hold the question in front of you, as if it has been asked by someone else who listens with great interest for your answer. They are in no hurry. Time means nothing. The person asking the question is neither critical, nor superior, nor bored. They are simply listening for the answer, just as you are.*

2   *And when answers arise that feel at least as if they are pointing you toward a resolution, they may be arising from the place within you that already knows.*

Asking the Existential Question

Unless you have a qualified teacher who authorizes you to continue, don't persist with "Who am I?" if you find it disturbing. Put it to one side. There will be plenty of time to return to it later if you wish. It can certainly be unsettling to discover that the person we thought we are is only a learned persona, rather than the true self. But don't worry – the true self (the term is inadequate) is nothing to fear. And since it is who we are, don't worry that it will slip away if you stop working on the koan.

But if you do wish to continue, recognize that the self you are seeking is the self that seeks. You are not, despite what some psychologists may say about "sub-personalities", a community of selves, some of whom ask questions and some of whom attempt to answer. By working through the meditations in this book, you will have recognized a still observer who watches the breathing, who visualizes, who observes thoughts and emotions, who asks existential questions. Who is this self? And why, over the years, have you, like the rest of us, lost sight of it?

In the West we are used to answers that can be expressed as words or formulas, answers that fit the questions asked no matter who asks them, answers that remain the same whether given to us by others or found out for ourselves. Existential questions are not quite so straightforward.

Staying with the Question

Like any koan, the question "Who am I?" can be used outside formal meditation. Either hold the question in the mind, with the same puzzled, almost amused attitude you adopt in meditation, or – using a method used by the great Hindu sage Ramana Maharshi – ask yourself "Who is it who is doing this action (whatever it is)?". "Who is it who is breathing?". Even "Who is it who is asking the question?".

After chanting the mantra of Amitabha Buddha ("Namu Amidha Butsu" or "Praise to Amitabha Buddha") for some years, the Buddhist sage Han Shan was still aware that he hadn't achieved the final realization of enlightenment. One day he met a hermit who advised him to ask "Who is it who is chanting the Buddha's mantra?". Han Shan took his advice, and became an enlightened master.

Is Someone There?

When the accretions learnt over the years are carefully stripped away, is there anybody or anything there? Some Western Buddhists might tell you there isn't. Others will tell you that "isn't" and "is" are only words, and must not be allowed to deceive us. They may also remind us that one of the key teachings in Buddhism is that "when the opposites arise, the Buddha mind is lost". Christians, Moslems and many Hindus will tell you that there is something there, a soul that is a creation or a reflection of God. And they will bid you realize that soul within yourself. Whatever path and whatever description appeals to you, follow that path and respond to that description. But remember that all the great traditions tell you not to listen only to descriptions given by others, but to "seek and you will find".

Simply listening to others is in fact akin to resting content with descriptions of a far country, without searching for it ourselves. Even if such descriptions are accurate, they are no substitute for direct experience. And the seeking is itself part of what we are seeking, though this is not always easy to grasp.

To seek for oneself is to seek for the meaning not behind your own life but behind all life. To seek for oneself is to seek for the creator of all life, for those infinite vistas that lie behind the narrow walls within which we too often confine ourselves.

MEDITATION 52: **Put Labels Aside**

The labels we associate with ourselves are true in a way. We use labels to define our names, nationalities and professions, and describe our personalities, attitudes and interests. Labels make it possible to function in modern society. However, they represent relative rather than absolute truths about us. Unless you dislike them, there is no reason to feel antipathy toward these labels. But don't mistake them for your real self. These meditations will help. But don't try them if you find them disturbing.

1 *Help yourself see beyond these labels by thinking back to a time when some of them didn't apply. Who were you then?*

2 *Think ahead to a time when you will have outgrown some of these labels. Who will you be then?*

3 *Think how your attitudes, interests and even personality traits have changed over the years. Can these be who you are?*

4 *Think of meditation sessions when the mind is calm and compare them with sessions when it is particularly busy. Who is the person sitting there in both these situations?*

5 *Reflect on times in meditation when thoughts and feelings no longer intrude. Who are you then?*

Continuing to Practise

Meditation is initially a novelty. Many people take to it quickly and report immediate benefits. They walk around with a calm smile on their faces, are warm and open and patient with people, and feel confident that their lives have changed for good (in both senses of the word). A few weeks later however the smile is less in evidence. Yes they're still meditating, but they're no longer doing so every day. Things have been so busy. They've had guests to stay. They've been working late on company reports. Holidays have intervened, and so on. Some weeks later still, they're no longer meditating, but yes, they intend to get back to their practice as soon as things ease off a little.

The last statement may be true. Having tasted the benefits of meditation, people do tend to return to it, even if intermittently, in the years that follow. But the earlier statements are also true. Many people start a meditation program, but not many keep to it. What is the reason, if meditation brings such clear initial benefits? Part of the problem is that the human mind craves novelty. After a while meditation may become stale. And the boredom mentioned in Chapter 2 also plays a part. What can be done to counteract this tendency to let meditation fall by the wayside?

One step is to find a good teacher. You can progress on your own. Hermits and wandering monks do so (although even they usually work with a teacher from time to time). But it is generally better to find and stay with a good teacher. (See the page opposite for some suggestions.)

Working with a group (perhaps led by your teacher) is also a great help. Group members encourage and help each other. Books are also a help, and there are many from which to choose. Another help (I would say essential) is to allow meditation to become part of daily life, instead of enclosing it within the half hour or so of your formal session. Mindfulness and the various meditations associated with it are meant to be practised as often as possible. Think of yourself as a meditator rather than as someone who does a bit of meditation when he or she feels like it.

A mantra is also a priceless asset. Your teacher may select one for you, or you may choose one for yourself. If nothing else, use a positive affirmation. Turn your mind to it as often as possible. If you like, use a *mala* also (a set of beads, 108 in number in the Eastern traditions) or a rosary, and finger each bead for each repetition of the mantra. You can also use the *mala* during sitting meditation, particularly at times when the mind is extra busy.

Try in addition to suit your meditation practice to your personality. Extroverts, who are more geared to outer experience, often find sitting meditation more difficult than do introverts, who are more attuned to inner states. If you are very extroverted, use active forms of meditation. Meditate for example while out

Finding a Teacher

The great majority of meditation teachers are associated with one or other of the spiritual traditions, particularly Hinduism and Buddhism. But a good teacher will never try to indoctrinate you in his or her spiritual beliefs. If you are not a member of their tradition, make this clear to your teacher and, if appropriate, the fact that you have no wish to become a member. He or she will understand, and will not turn you away.

The value of teachers grounded in the great traditions (increasingly there are good teachers from within the Christian faith as well, and Sufi groups are becoming more common) is that you know they will have had a good training, and will be answerable to their traditions for their behaviour. Don't regard your teacher as an oracle, but while working with them carefully follow their guidance. If you dislike this guidance, find another teacher.

Going on Retreat

Retreats are an opportunity to devote yourself to meditation over a period of a few days (longer as you become more experienced). Usually your retreat will be organized by your teacher, and attended mainly by members of your own group.

Make sure you know in advance what the retreat entails. Your first experience should be demanding but not overwhelming. How long will the meditation sessions be? (No longer than half an hour for beginners.) How many sessions will there be in the day? (Be guided by your teacher, but five or six are usually appropriate to start with.) How will the rest of the time be used? Will the retreat be in silence? How basic is the accommodation?

Make sure as well that you can "come down" after the retreat, when you return to daily life. This can be difficult. Retreats are a time out from normal living. Discuss this with your teacher.

jogging or walking or cycling or when swimming, keeping the mind centred on the rhythmic action of the body. Many sportsmen and women report achieving a particular kind of high while engaged in their sport that is very similar to the altered states achieved at some levels of meditation. Meditate while gardening, putting your awareness in the activity rather than in your own thoughts. Do the same while engaging in your favourite hobby. Buddhism speaks of a "Zen state", in which the mind is so fully absorbed in an activity that it loses all sense of time and place and self. Modern psychology recognizes the value of this state, which is sometimes referred to as "flow".

If you find your meditation has become sporadic, ask yourself why. Don't be put off by excuses about being too busy. In life we tend to find time for the things we really want to do. Go back to your meditation diary and remind yourself of the benefits recorded there. Write down your resolution to keep practising. Outline the details of a program to which you will be able to keep. Note the things that could get in the way of this program, and how you plan to overcome them.

Finally, think deeply about the questions that may have brought you into meditation in the first place. Questions about the meaning of life, the existence of a spiritual dimension, the nature of the self, the mind and the soul. Resolve to keep seeking answers, and using meditation to help you in your search.

Working with a Group and a Teacher

Groups usually gather around teachers, and a good group follows the teacher's guidance without too much dissent. Much of course depends upon the teacher. There is an old story of a man who goes to the master and asks what he must do if he becomes his pupil. The master tells him. The man listens in alarm at the amount of dedication involved, and decides to ask instead how he can become a teacher. The role of the teacher may look easier, but the teacher carries a great responsibility for the group. In Buddhism it is said that he or she takes on the karma of the pupils – certainly he or she must be careful not to lead them astray.

In the old days individuals often had to prove themselves before the master would accept them. There are tales of people sitting outside the master's dwelling for months, even years before they proved themselves sufficiently dedicated to become pupils. Things are less severe now, but a degree of commitment to the teacher and to the group is still necessary. And although group membership brings great benefits, it can often cause unexpected problems, particularly on retreats. It seems that the human mind has a certain capacity for irritation and resentment, and if this is not satisfied by the usual friction of daily life, it looks for other outlets. The abbot of a monastery once told me of the great difficulty he had sitting near a fellow monk – especially at meals and in the meditation hall – who kept sniffing. No matter how insignificant, small things like this can get out of all proportion in group work.

The meditator is always told to use these irritations as a learning process. If irritations and resentments arise with no good cause, what do these irritations and resentments represent? Why and from where do they arise? How can they be put aside? Similar irritations and resentments may arise toward a teacher. He or she may at times seem insufferably smug, or too demanding, or to favour some pupils over others. One teacher with whom I worked years ago travelled abroad to study with a highly respected master, and on his return told me of his anger when the master corrected aspects of his practice. He caught himself rejecting the idea that the master really knew anything about practice. It was only when he had worked through this initial stage of hostility that the learning process – with its manifold benefits – could begin.

You may find that another challenge when working with a group is being asked for advice by others. When this happens it is all too easy to begin to cast yourself in the role of a teacher. Resist the temptation. It may be flattering to think that others value our guidance, but never step outside what you know. In meditation, a little knowledge can at times be a dangerous thing. Help others by all means, but be careful not to mislead them.

Conclusion

A highly respected master was once asked what advice he would give to someone considering taking up meditation. His answer was "Start – and continue". After working through this book, my hope is that you have started, and that you will now continue. And remember to keep meditation in your heart without allowing it to go to your head. Don't fall into the error of thinking that meditation is something that you do, and that the benefits are due to your own efforts. No good gardener would imagine that beautiful flowers are a result of his or her efforts. And like a good gardener, our role in meditation is to establish the conditions in which results can be obtained. We are no more responsible for these results than we are for the fact that we are alive.

Meditation therefore requires humility. Results arise because that is the nature of the mind that we have been given. The mind that reveals itself once we cease to obscure it with the fog of unnecessary mental distraction. Of equal importance to humility is the ability to stay grounded. It is possible, when meditation appears to be going well, to become rather unworldly. The daily concerns of work and family may fade into the background. Instead of becoming more focused and effective in daily life, one may become detached, even indifferent. All that seems to matter may be the realization of spiritual non-physical realms. This unworldly state of mind is a sure sign that meditation, despite appearances, is not going well. Meditation is about your ordinary life, not about escape from it. This ordinary life is realized as the expression of the ultimate reality from which everything arises and to which everything one day returns. Sometimes this realization is expressed as the sacredness of daily living. Zen Buddhism in particular stresses that the mind should always be present within the immediacy of experience. When working work, when resting rest, when sleeping sleep. The present moment is not separate from any spiritual dimensions which you know to exist.

So don't allow meditation to take you away from the world. Rather, allow meditation to help you appreciate the world, to feel gratitude for family and friends, for nature with its abundance, for animals and the plants and the trees. Feel gratitude too for inanimate things, for the beauty of distant mountains and running water, for the minerals in the earth that help produce the food we eat. Above all perhaps, for sunlight, which illuminates and warms, for the sun itself – the perfect symbol of sacrifice, for in sustaining all life on this Earth the sun itself is slowly dying.

In this gratitude you are also expressing recognition of the creator of the cosmos, however you conceive the reality of this creator. Finally, you are expressing gratitude for your own precious human life, and for a mind through which the created world is able continually to express itself.

Further Reading

Both UK and US publishers are given where applicable.

- There is a large number of helpful books on meditation. The author's own *Learn to Meditate* and *Learn Zen Meditation* (both published by Duncan Baird) should prove useful, as should his *The Meditator's Handbook* (Thorsons).

- Among the many relatively recent books that can be highly recommended are Amadeo Solé-Leris *Tranquillity and Insight* (Rider/Pariyatti), Kamalashila *Meditation: The Buddhist Way of Tranquility and Insight* (Windhorse/Weatherhill), Achaan Chah *A Still Forest Pool* (Quest/Theosophical), Rod Bucknell and Chris Kang (editors) *The Meditative Way* (RoutledgeCurzon) and Alan Wallace *The Bridge of Quiescence* (Open Court).

- Advice on how to work with children in meditation is given by David Fontana and Ingrid Slack *Teaching Meditation to Children* (Thorsons).

- For guidance on how to undertake a meditation retreat, the best book known to me is Roger Housden's *Retreat: Time Apart for Silence and Solitude* (Thorsons).

- Those who wish to follow up on current medical research on the healing power of meditation, prayer and distant healing, and on other aspects of the mind-body relationship could not do better than Herbert Benson *Timeless Healing: The Power and Biology of Belief* (Simon and Schuster/Scribner), Bill Moyers (editor) *Healing and the Mind* (Doubleday), Daniel Goleman and Joel Gurin (editors) *Mind Body Medicine* (Consumer Reports Books), and two books by Larry Dossey, *Reinventing Medicine* (HarperCollins) and *Healing Beyond the Body: Medicine and the Infinite Reach of the Mind* (Time Warner/Shambhala).

- An interesting survey of altered states of consciousness during sporting activities is Michael Murphy and Rhea White *In the Zone: Transcendent Experience in Sports* (Penguin USA).

Index